PRAISE FOR SOUPELINA

"Soupelina has healing power! I was feeling under the weather with a terrible sinus headache and tried several other natural methods to relieve it but was still in pain and nauseous. One full day of the Veggie Healing Broth brought me back to life. The combination of cayenne pepper, ginger, and Asian veggies among the freshest ingredients make for an amazing broth that soothes the tummy, opens up the breathing passages, loosens phlegm, and eases the headache."

—Maria, record industry executive, Los Angeles

"Soupelina's 3-day cleanse was just what I needed to lose a couple pounds while not sacrificing my life for delicious food. I have tried juice cleanses on several occasions and always found that I would be so hungry that I spent all three days obsessing about not being able to eat. The soup cleanse was so much more filling. I had more energy and a clearer head than when I juiced. The soups were so flavorful and downright fantastic."

—Pam, skin care consultant, Encino

"I incorporate Soupelina into my daily dietary regimen. I live a very busy lifestyle and Soupelina is a quick, convenient supplemental resource I use to get in the nutrients needed to keep me energized and nourished all day long. I take my soups with me everywhere I go."

—Chaz, celebrity hairstylist, Los Angeles

"For someone who has to do gluten-free, it can be a real challenge finding great, healthy soups that don't come from a can or a box. I tried Elina's soups and I was hooked. Elina cares about her clients and their overall health. She is making people healthier one soup at a time."

—Cathy, pet nutrition consultant, Studio City

"I started eating Soupelina over a year ago to help boost my energy levels and add extra nutrition to my diet. Not only are the soups delicious (Kale-ifornia Dreamin' is my favorite), but they are packed with so many vitamins and healing nutrients that I feel energized and most importantly, nourished, after eating a bowl. Incorporating these soups into my routine has made me feel better than ever before."

—Terena, writer, Los Angeles

"I've been vegan for a while and it isn't easy to find delicious soups, especially with clean ingredients. I wasn't feeling well, so I decided to do a weeklong cleanse and I loved every soup I had. I never felt deprived or hungry; it was great to know I was eating something truly healthy. Within just a few days I started feeling much better from all of the healing soups. I never ended up getting sick and I felt even better after the cleanse than I had before."

— *Cori, hair artist, Silver Lake*

"I just completed my 5-day Soupelina cleanse and I feel amazing! I didn't know that losing 7 pounds in just 5 days would be that easy! I'm going to keep this up because I've never felt better. Not only was I able to finally fit into my skinny jeans, I'm better balanced, can finally concentrate on my work and kids, my skin is glowing and I feel so empowered! Thank you, Soupelina, for giving me my old energy and body back. Good-bye, fatigue! Hello, a better me!"

—*Donna, homemaker, Los Angeles*

"I've been struggling with high cholesterol for years and tried many medications. Nothing worked until I tried Elina's healing soup cleanse. I have to admit, I was skeptical but wanted to try anyway because I enjoy soups. When my doctor told me that my levels were good for the first time in years just after one week of souping, I couldn't believe it. Eating healthy does work and it does change your life."

—*Stacy, retired, Los Angeles*

"I don't know how Elina makes her soups so flavorful without what I was use to, tons of animal fat. Her soups are filling, delicious; the perfect comfort food. I have incorporated her knowledge of healthy eating into my diet and I am seeing results. Thank you!"

—*Adina, actress, Los Angeles*

"Soupelina's soups are of the highest quality ingredients available. They taste great, make you feel great and don't even resemble soups you get elsewhere. Ever feel like your head is going to explode from the salt in other soups? Not here! The nutritional value is through the roof! Despite the fact that Soupelina soups are 100% vegan and organic and that I am a sworn meat eater and a body builder, I still love them!"

—*Jason, personal fitness trainer, body builder*

SOUPELINA'S
SOUP CLEANSE

made with love

SOUPELINA'S
SOUP CLEANSE

**Plant-Based Soups and Broths to Heal Your Body,
Calm Your Mind, and Transform Your Life**

ELINA FUHRMAN

founder of Soupelina

Photography by Pär Bengtsson
Direction by Randy Price
Styling by Angela Yeung

Da Capo
∞
LIFE
LONG

A Member of the Perseus Books Group

Copyright © 2016 by Elina Fuhrman Living LLC
Soupelina(tm) is a trademark of Elina Fuhrman

Patent Pending. The pending patent application covers soup compositions including ingredients uniquely selected for particular nutritional benefits and recipes for making soup compositions to maximize the nutritional benefit of the compositions.

Photography by Pär Bengtsson
Direction by Randy Price
Styling by Angela Yeung
Designed by Nancy Singer
Cover design by Madeline Fuhrman

Editorial production by Marrathon Production Services. www.marrathon.net
Set in 10.75 point Adobe Caslon Pro

Cataloging-in-Publication data for this book is available from the Library of Congress.

First Da Capo Press edition 2016
ISBN: 978-0-7382-1888-5 (hardcover)
ISBN: 978-0-7382-1889-2 (e-book)

Published by Da Capo Press
A Member of the Perseus Books Group
www.dacapopress.com

Note: The information in this book is true and complete to the best of our knowledge. This book is intended only as an informative guide for those wishing to know more about health issues. In no way is this book intended to replace, countermand, or conflict with the advice given to you by your own physician. The ultimate decision concerning care should be made between you and your doctor. We strongly recommend you follow his or her advice. Information in this book is general and is offered with no guarantees on the part of the authors or Da Capo Press. The authors and publisher disclaim all liability in connection with the use of this book.

Da Capo Press books are available at special discounts for bulk purchases in the U.S. by corporations, institutions, and other organizations. For more information, please contact the Special Markets Department at the Perseus Books Group, 2300 Chestnut Street, Suite 200, Philadelphia, PA, 19103, or call (800) 810-4145, ext. 5000, or e-mail special.markets@perseusbooks.com.

BANG

10 9 8 7 6 5 4 3

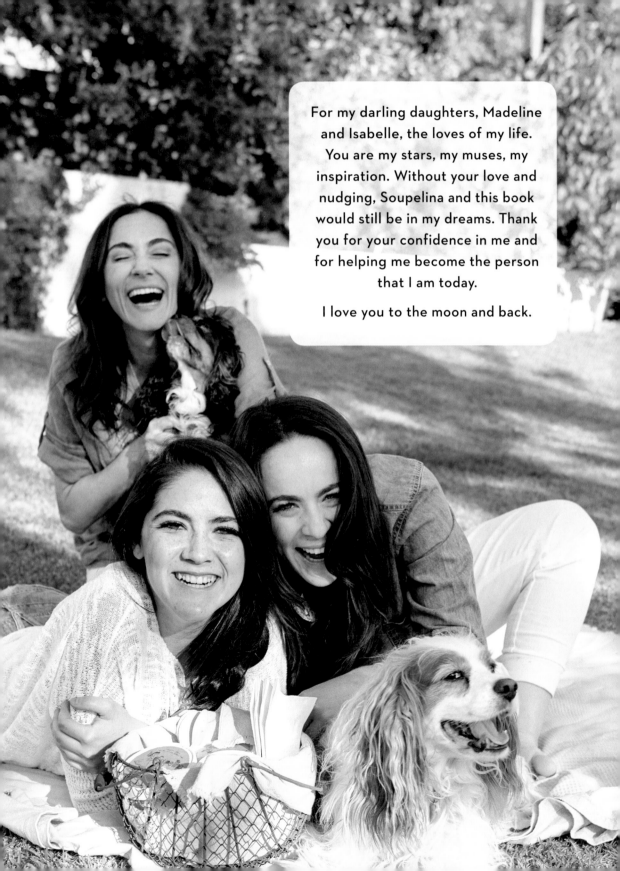

For my darling daughters, Madeline and Isabelle, the loves of my life. You are my stars, my muses, my inspiration. Without your love and nudging, Soupelina and this book would still be in my dreams. Thank you for your confidence in me and for helping me become the person that I am today.

I love you to the moon and back.

Contents

CONTENTS   ix

8
_____

I AM DONE WITH THE CLEANSE; NOW WHAT? 205

Continuing the Cleanse | Breaking the Cleanse | Soup Cleanse Seasonally | Keep the
Toxins Out of Your Kitchen and Your Body

9
_____

LISTEN TO YOUR GUT 215

What Is Your Gut Telling You? | Gut Balance with Dr. Gerard Mullin, MD
gastrointerologist, nutritionist, gut microbiome authority | Dr. Gerard Mullin's
Prescription for Gut Health | Younger Skin with Dr. Harold Lancer, MD, Fellow of the
American Academy of Dermatology | Allow Your Food to Create Your Glow from the
Inside Out: Dr. Lancer's Rx for Great Skin

Foreword

Congratulations! By purchasing this book you've taken an important first step toward better health through nutrition. In the last few years there has been an awakening across the medical community regarding the fundamental importance of nutrition as a key component of health. It is now generally accepted that imbalances of nutrition are pivotal to the root causes of many common diseases that our modern society faces today. Likewise, the jury is in regarding prevention, and the preponderance of scientific studies support the notion that the best nutritional armor is a plant-based diet.

As a physician board-certified in internal medicine, geriatric medicine, and integrative/holistic medicine, I can attest to true transformations in my patients and in myself personally from the miracle of plant-based foods. The integrative approach that my colleagues and I practice has helped many patients with chronic health issues, and the combination of nutrition, exercise, appropriate use of medication, mind-body techniques, and spiritual health practices together constitute the foundation of our integrative health model. We consider proper nutrition to be at the core of all of this. However, we recognize that for patients, applying a correct nutrition plan in real life takes courage, commitment, willpower, and steadfastness.

The industrialization of the food supply has brought us great convenience. Unfortunately, such convenience comes at a price. The influence of big business, cultural trends, and market forces have all contributed powerfully to the way people eat. So, in many ways, the deck is stacked against the average person who just wants to be healthy and to eat as healthily as possible. To make matters worse, diet fads and weight-loss schemes are only too often confused with nutrition. Consider the magnitude of the weight-loss industry within a culture that glorifies "thin" in the face of a seemingly unstoppable obesity epidemic. People looking for dietary and nutritional advice face a mind-boggling array of food choices and misguided "expert" opinions, making it almost impossible to know which path to take. With all of that in mind, it is my personal pleasure to write the foreword for this book.

When Elina Fuhrman decided to explore the world of healing nutrition with the intention of creating tools to help people eat for their health, I knew there was no better person to synthesize the available information and come up with a practical plan. The result was her wonderful book on healing soups. The formulations of these soups were guided by nutritional science with the goal of providing a clear source of information for the achievement of good health. The carefully selected nutrients in them are intended to target important functions, such as immune health, blood sugar balance, anti-inflammatory activity, and gastrointestinal health. Besides the recipes proper, Elina takes the opportunity to inform readers in sections on digestion, Ayurvedic medicine, Chinese medicine, homeopathy, and naturopathy.

The book addresses important questions people often have about such topics as sugar and its role in cancer and other diseases. What foods that Americans eat regularly may be dangerous and potentially cancer forming? How important is it to eat organic produce or avoid GMOs? Can we really reverse disease with proper nutrition? How do nutritional soups contribute to better health? How do different types of hot and raw soups and broths support cleansing and detoxification? Why is detoxification important? What's the relationship between a healthy gut and a healthy body, and how can soups help with that? What are the biggest mistakes we make that make us sick? Some of the answers will surprise you, some will seem logical, and some will make you angry when you realize how difficult the food industry has made it to eat and be healthy.

In conclusion, the practical challenges of changing one's nutrition are often the most daunting aspects of a lifestyle change. With the ubiquitous question "What do I eat now?" at the top of everyone's list, this book provides a clear, practical, effective, and fun guide of the what, when, why, and how. I am convinced that Elina's enthusiasm, love, and strong desire to help

Soupelina

people achieve better health represent the true force contained in this book. It will empower those who seek help in improving their health, not to mention their taste buds and the enjoyment of food. Bon appétit!

Anthony J. Bazzan, MD, FACN, ABIHM
Director, Functional & Wellness Sciences Institute
Codirector, The Great Life Executive Health Program at the Myrna Brind
Center of Integrative Medicine, Thomas Jefferson University
Coauthor of the popular book, *The Great Life Makeover*

Introduction

MY WALK INTO WELLNESS

I was lying on a cold bathroom floor, crying my eyes out and begging to survive. *If I do*, I was pleading, *I will tell everyone what helped me.* I was praying for a miracle because that's all I knew how to do.

I had just been diagnosed with breast cancer.

The words alone evoke images of a death sentence and thinking about treatments made me feel even worse. *I will never be whole again*, I cried. I mourned my life and hoped the diagnosis was a mistake.

Surely the docs looked at someone else's mammogram, I thought. *I'm certain it wasn't my tissue they tested*, I told myself. I was convinced that they would figure out the mishap; it was just a matter of time. How could they not? I was healthy! I had no family history of any cancer. I ate well, I exercised, I took care of myself, I breastfed my kids when they were babies. I was happy at work as a journalist, traveling to exotic countries, seeking out the best the world has to offer and writing about it for magazines and newspapers.

But the more tests the doctors ran, the more concerned they got. I was "lucky," they told me, I'd "caught it early"—but the bad news was that the cancer was aggressive and growing fast, so they wanted me to do everything medically possible to stop it in its tracks. Except that I didn't want to. The treatment choices I faced didn't support the way I wanted to live. So, I put on my investigative journalist shoes, hit the road, and took a walk into the wellness.

My healing pilgrimage connected me with some of the most knowledgeable and well-known people in the medical community and what I learned shocked me. I found out that cancer is not some kind of mysterious disease we have no control over. I learned that there was no medical cure, but rather, **health is a choice**, and my daily choices, whether I realize it or not, were making a direct impact on my health.

When I showed up at the office of Dr. Kristi Funk, the not-yet-famous breast surgeon, she took one look at my MRI and asked whether something stressful happened in my life five years prior. She then gently suggested I see her friend, a renowned herbalist and acupuncturist Dr. Mao Shing Ni for answers. Dr. Mao asked me about my unspoken emotions, told me my cancer "wasn't physical," and promised that I had a lot of work ahead of me. Dr. Funk and Dr. Mao were the perfect East-meets-West medical team to help guide me to my optimum health.

Dr. Mao introduced me to Chinese medicine; Dr. Funk cited scientific research but also hinted that I look into Ayurveda and connected me with other like-minded physicians, such as my oncologist, Dr. Philomena McAndrew; OB-GYN and clinical Ayurvedic specialist, Dr. Susanne Gilberg-Lenz; and my integrative GP, Dr. Jennifer Sudarsky. I became a voracious student of all things health and wellness, integrating ancient healing traditions to transform a cancer diagnosis into vibrant living. Interestingly enough, food was at the cornerstone of it all.

But what about soups? Well, soups became a form of self-love and comfort as I changed the way I ate, gave up all meat and dairy, and turned to plant-based foods. I like the way that sounds, more than the V-word. Yes, I'm talking about becoming a vegan. I've been fortunate to travel the world and enjoy culinary creations from (plus cook alongside) the most-celebrated chefs in Paris, Bangkok, and Capetown, and I had a hard time settling for steamed veggies and rice. *There's got to be a way to bring the world to my dinner table and certainly into a healing bowl of soup*, I thought. And that's exactly what I did.

Even though my delicious soups began as a way to heal myself, they became so much more than that. I wasn't looking for a business, but I found myself drawn to spending days in the kitchen, putting the love I felt into every pot. Finding your calling is a funny thing. You don't get to choose it; it chooses you. And no matter what I did or didn't do, one serendipitous encounter after the other led me down this totally unexpected, unplanned path. I realized that I had to do this. Didn't I promise the universe that if I figured out a way to heal myself, I would tell everyone what I did?

I developed a collection of soups, conceived all-natural sustainable packaging, and launched the Soupelina brand (Soup + Elina!). This was my gift to friends and like-minded people, a way to share the gourmet magic and what I learned about wellness and healing. But I had no clue that Soupelina would open the door to a growing community of people who are passionate about plant-based food that is not only healthy but lip-smacking delicious as well. As the e-mails from happy customers began flowing with stories of healing, lost weight, increased energy, and better mood, I knew that this was no longer just my own passion project; I realized that I could help people heal themselves.

This book is my love letter to life born from a cancer diagnosis that pushed me into a healthy obsession with, well, health. Lucky for me, it couldn't have happened at a better time.

I wrote *Soupelina's Soup Cleanse* because I believe in just that: a healthy and happy life can be lived through good soup. I hope to inspire you to tie on your favorite apron, and through cooking your favorite soups from this book, unleash your soup-per powers.

Healthy plant-based, veg-centered eating and wellness are taking the world by storm, infusing the media and pop culture and raising a new generation of healthy eaters. I'm so very proud to be a voice in this wellness revolution that I believe will transform the world and our health.

Soup has been so good to me. *Soupelina's Soup Cleanse* is a celebration of all the soups that brought me vibrant health, overwhelming happiness, and not to mention, a new career. I hope they'll bring that much to you.

Now get ready to transform your own health as you embark on a souping journey with me. Let's do some good! Soup up!

xo Elina

1

SOUP UP

What Is a Soup Cleanse?

I love when my friends call me "the soup guru." How cool is that? But I also have another title: I'm the Soup Cleanse inventor. I created the Soup Cleanse after learning how slowly simmered organic soups can heal the body. A believer in cleansing, I knew I had to rid my body of toxins in order to kick cancer in the butt. I also wanted the energetic, vital, joyful, and healthy me again.

Besides, I was so tired of scrolling through Instagram photos of just about everyone in LA "juice cleansing" that I wanted to shake things up. Don't get me wrong; I love juicing but you know what goes on during juice cleansing: You feel tired, you feel dizzy, you feel hungry, your blood sugar goes up and down because of all the sugary fruits mixed in with the greens. And by the time you are done, you are so ready for a juicy cheeseburger.

I needed a different kind of cleanse and since soup was what was up in my house, I announced that I was soup cleansing. Mind you, that was back in 2011. Nobody knew what the heck I was talking about. I would get those suspicious looks along with occasional nods of understanding. Soup was not something people associated with healthy eating, cleanses, and diets: Soups were loaded with sodium, cream, and all those unpronounceable ingredients.

Like a mad scientist, I would spend hours in the kitchen, injecting sparks of my newfound culinary creativity and healing juju into souping, creating my one-of-a-kind organic blends with nothing more than fresh veggies, herbs, spices, and occasional legumes. I would make up witty names for my soups, mainly because they were so different from anything I could find.

Having soup for breakfast, lunch, and dinner was much better than rice and veggies, and way more satisfying than juices. I never felt hungry. Quite the opposite: I felt nourished, comforted, and loved. But I would crave a little something between meals; that's when Dr. Mao told me about the healing power of broths. Having hot broths for snacks was a godsend. I would load them with fresh herbs and sprinkle them with cayenne for a kick. They were feisty, tasty, and I couldn't seem to get enough. The good news: I could have them all day long!

Soups didn't make me feel like I was missing anything. What they did was make me feel more energized, focused, happier, and brighter. When I completed my first soup cleanse, I felt better than I've ever felt in my life. For the first time I didn't feel stressed, my tummy and my mind were calm, my poo was regular, and I had lost 5 pounds. My skin was glowing, my hair was silkier, and I couldn't stop smiling. And another thing happened: People started telling me I looked younger. So clearly, I was onto something.

The concept that soup heals your body and your life is not new. For generations people have enjoyed soup to nourish and heal, and they have also searched for the perfect soup to cure what ails them. Somehow, our fast-paced modern lives turned much-beloved soups into sodium- and preservative-laden concoctions that were not only tasteless but also bad for you.

Soupelina's Soup Cleanse is a powerful detox program that will give you extra energy, provide all your body's necessary fiber, improve digestion, sharpen your mind, eliminate stress, reduce inflammation, and also keep you feeling full, warm, and loved. The indulgent yet virtuous recipes in this book will empower your life and help you in creating a roadmap to your own healing and inner peace.

I also promise you a culinary adventure with style, texture, and layers of flavor and glamour, because that's how I roll! So, whether you are an experienced soup gourmand or a novice, you will notice a difference in your health within days. And that change will surely spill into the rest of your life—your spirit, your relationships, your home, and the planet.

Soupelina

COOKING LESSONS

I grew up in the former Soviet Union, and both my mother and grandmother always cooked. I don't remember ever eating in restaurants unless we were on vacation or at a few wedding parties my family was invited to attend. We always had gatherings with family and friends, and there was always lots of food on the table.

My mom used to joke that even in college I wouldn't know how to boil a pot of water. She would send me weekly meal packages with overnight train attendants. She was so ahead of the time: This was the original food delivery, Soviet style. I didn't start cooking until I got married. I wanted to be like my mother and show off my cooking skills, so I would write letters to her asking for recipes and then attempt to make them in our kitchen.

But it was travel that changed the way I saw cooking. As a travel journalist, I ate and drank through great cities and towns, five-star restaurants and little dives, discovering great food and writing about it. I spent time with chefs, touring kitchens and picking up a trick or two. I began to develop my own style and I took cooking classes in restaurants around the world, from France to South Africa, Japan, India, Thailand, and the Caribbean.

So, naturally when I stopped eating meat and dairy, I just couldn't give up on the fun. I wanted to re-create the flavors; I wanted my food to be exciting yet nourishing and full of flavor, but easy to make. I loved that soups had history and culture, but also had sass and elegance. Soup became my go-to: It fit my style and cooking philosophy but also provided a delicious and healing meal.

Soup also helped me find awareness of my body, emotions, and daily choices; tune into my deepest thoughts; and create a balance in my life.

Since changing what I eat and how I live, my body and mind are now healthier, stronger, and more empowered than I ever imagined possible. I prove my own point every day and the proof is definitely in the soup.

Soup Cleanse Basics and How to Use This Book

Soup cleansing enables your body to go naturally into detox mode while replenishing your body with essential minerals, increasing circulation, and reducing inflammation. The recipes I created include unique combinations of herbs and spices with cleansing powers that support the detoxification of the bowel and urinary systems, skin, sweat glands, liver, and kidneys. This holistic combination of herbs and spices with specific veggies and legumes in my soups create a natural balance and cleanse your body's purification systems at once.

Soups are great for detox because they don't require as much energy to digest, freeing your body to heal and at the same time providing you with all the necessary fiber and nutrients.

I like to think of the Soup Cleanse as a feast, a holiday for your body, and the ultimate indulgence.

Most of the soups in this book are simple to make. All of them are made from scratch, using the freshest organic ingredients. The recipes are organized by the type of soups: blended, chunky, broths, and raw soups. All the soups are vegan, made from some familiar ingredients and some exotic ones, too. I like discovering new veggies, spices, and herbs and creating soups that not only are bursting with flavor but have medicinal and healing properties, too. Some examples of this are The Truffle with Asparagus Soup, Magic Turmeric Broth, and Cure for the Common Kohlrabi Soup.

I almost always add a pinch of cayenne or a squeeze of lime or lemon to the soup to bring flavors together. I love dressing soups and broths with fresh herbs, sprouts, or a teeny drizzle of herbal oil when I serve them. It's as much for the beauty as it is to complete the soup. You won't go out to a fancy dinner wearing no accessories. I never get tired of the "ta-da" moment, when the soup comes alive. It's always exciting!

Soupelina

To get the most out of your cleanse, it helps to cleanse seasonally to stay in tune with nature. If you've never cleansed before, start with a 3-Day Seasonal Cleanse. If you are one of my Expert Cleansers, challenge yourself by adding wheatgrass shots and enemas to get the most out of your efforts. Regardless of what you choose, all cleanses are designed to fit into your daily routine. Whether this is your first cleanse or your tenth, each experience is unique. The main goal is to peel away the layers and shed old patterns as you move toward a new you. This not only relates to your food choices, but emotions, relationships, career, and family. Your life is about to take a beautiful turn.

The Soup Cleanse is a time for your body to relax and nourish itself. Be gentle and kind to yourself during the cleanse, don't engage in rigorous workouts, and avoid stress. Observe your stressors and practice relaxation. Spend five minutes upon waking and five minutes before bedtime visualizing something that makes you extremely happy and run a mental list of things you are grateful for.

Why Soup Cleanse?

Move over, green smoothies and fruit-loaded juices! Who isn't tired of another variation on kale, banana, or coconut? We all know that in today's world, looking and feeling well is the measure of a life best lived, so what are we to do? The Soup Cleanse is the solution not just to a slimmer you, but the healthy and sexy you, without aches, pains, and that afternoon slump; with glowing, clear skin (good-bye acne!), PMS-free months (who came up with PMS anyway?), and without any stress (is that even possible?).

For centuries, doctors and healers in every culture have recommended various holistic purification rituals to remove toxins, create well-being, and balance the body. There is a good reason for that. When you eliminate heavy carbs, animal proteins, sugars, preservatives, chemical additives, and artificial stimulants from your daily diet, you give your digestive and detoxification organs a much-needed rest from the day-to-day attack of nutritional stress. By introducing easily digestible wholesome organic soups, you not only nourish your body, but also give it time to repair and restore the disease-fighting functions of your immune system. The cleanse also rebuilds the fat-burning functions of your metabolism and the energy-boosting functions of your nerves and master glands. The end result is more energy, less body fat, a stronger immune system, and better health.

If you are into health and wellness and the food that makes you feel healthy, this is your cup of soup. This book is a road map to your own soup-making journey of self-empowerment, vibrant health, a lean body, and happiness.

Inspired by my travels around the world, I created these recipes with variety, taste, and therapeutic value in mind. But they are also soup-er easy to prepare and rely on real food and ingredients, rather than specialist, often difficult-to-source vegan substitutes. After just one cleanse, your energy levels will be off the charts, your mind will be crisp and clear, your stress will be gone and you will feel as if you can do anything! Imagine what will happen if you stick with it and continue to incorporate soups into your daily life?!

Soupelina

WHY COOKING VEGGIES IS BETTER

I love raw, but I've come to believe that cooking my veggies is best and here is why.

+ You eat more veggies.

Think about it: An entire bag of spinach becomes a tiny portion the moment you steam it. One bowl of soup can be two bags! The amount of nutrition you are getting is mind-blowing!

+ It's easier to digest.

Cooking softens the fibers, warms the food, and helps your body digest everything. When we're eating raw, our digestive tract has to warm the veggies inside in order to digest them.

+ Cooked veggies have more yang.

Yin and yang are a fundamental part of Traditional Chinese Medicine; yin is negative and dark, while yang is positive and bright. I trust ancient medicine and Chinese Medicine believes that more yang (which is what cooked veggies provide) is better for healing, mostly because toxins are yin. Also, as much as I love juicing, it's all yin; that's why I'm always cold when I juice even for a day.

+ You absorb minerals easier.

You will learn more about the gut later in the book, and how important absorption of minerals is to our digestion and health. True, cooking destroys a few vitamins, but it makes the minerals much easier to absorb.

+ Cooked veggies balance doshas.

You will become more familiar with Ayurvedic principles of eating in the next chapter. Raw foods are considered cold and harder to digest. Raw soups are an exception only if they include warming spices and herbs to counteract the cold. The spices is what enhances the digestion that otherwise raw foods lack.

+ Cooked veggies have fewer bacteria.

Even organic veggies can have them. Wash your veggies carefully, but cooking them makes things so much simpler.

SOUP CLEANSE
Summary

EAT

Every day, eat one soup for each meal: breakfast, lunch, and dinner. For optimal results, eat soups every three hours throughout the day to keep your metabolism revved up. Each soup portion should be 12 to 16 ounces. You can cook the soups for your cleanse on a weekend and pack them up to take with you. Do not skip meals. Eat your first soup within thirty minutes of waking. Do not eat within three hours of going to sleep.

SNACK

Snack on prepared broths dressed with fresh herbs, sprouts, sesame seeds, and veggies of your choice. If you feel like something extra, indulge in raw cucumbers, celery, radishes, or cauliflower, as your heart desires. You can have fermented veggies and/or a handful of raw sprouted unsalted sunflower or pumpkin seeds with your broths.

DRINK

Start your day with a cup of hot water and lemon juice from half a lemon immediately upon waking, to flush the detox organs—kidneys, liver, and skin. Drink lots of water, lemon water, Rejuvelak (fermented quinoa drink, see page 190), or green or fresh herbal tea throughout the day and during cravings. Drink plenty of water between meals and especially during the workouts. Do not drink water during meals, for optimum digestion.

Soupelina

ELIMINATE

You should be having bowel movements at least twice per day while detoxing. After several days of cleansing, the walls of the colon release a buildup of plaque, allowing the body to maximize absorption of nutrition. You may experience a release of stored emotions and memories and a heightened sense of clarity. It's a good idea to consider colon hydrotherapy to aid your detox.

REST

Give yourself the time and space to rest as some major cleaning and healing is happening in your body; your body is very busy on a cellular level. Your energy levels will fluctuate on a day-to-day and moment-to-moment basis. Listen to your gut. If you feel tired, take it easy. If you feel a surge of energy, do what you need to express it.

AVOID

Avoid coffee, any sugar, including fruits, sodas/diet sodas, animal protein, dairy, alcohol, wheat, nicotine, processed foods, and fried foods.

CONSIDER

For Expert cleansers, incorporate wheatgrass and turmeric shots into your detox to increase the benefits.

SLEEP

Consider this cleanse your wake-up call: Stop worrying about how many hours of sleep you get, but start focusing on how well you sleep. As soon as you feel drowsy in the evening, don't put it off for even thirty minutes; go to bed or you can miss your body's natural sleep cycle.

2

THE BALANCING ACT

What Is Healthy Digestion?

I know I promised you culinary glamour, but let's take a moment and talk about something we often gloss over: our poop. Do you poop every day? If the answer is no, then you are full of you know what.

We all poop. But do you poop with a library of magazines in your loo, with squeezing, straining, even grunting, or meditation? Do you rely on coffee to get you going? Is your poo chunky or soft like peanut butter?

Because if you are not pooping right, something is up. A healthy body depends on healthy digestion, and healthy digestion produces healthy poop. You can spend hours in privacy Googling the photos and checking how your turds stack up, but what you absolutely have to know is that our

digestion is responsible for absolutely every ache, pain, and disease that is not accident-related. And what's even crazier is that we have known this for centuries! Hippocrates, that famous Greek physician and father of modern medicine we all love to quote, said that "all diseases begin in the gut" back in the third century BCE! So, why has it taken us this long to finally start believing that?

Digestion 101 is something we are all kind of familiar with: It's a process of extracting nutrients from the food we eat, breaking down fats, proteins, and carbohydrates and then discharging the residue from this process as feces. It starts in your mouth—your mom was right when she told you to chew your food properly—and ends in the bowl . . . the toilet bowl, that is.

When you eat wonderful organic foods, they go in, spread the goodness to your cells, and come out in a beautiful package. But sadly, this is not the case for so many. What goes in doesn't always come out. It's true that our body is designed to cleanse itself daily, but our fast-paced modern lives and exposure to an increasing number of harmful and toxic substances have all compromised our natural abilities to eliminate it all. Many of us have impacted colons from years of eating too much meat, dairy, processed and baked foods, pesticides, prescription drugs, and the list goes on. What that means is that you might have up to 10 extra pounds lodged in your colon. How gross is that?

The walls of your small intestine are lined with tiny villi that create the greatest surface area for food absorption. When you eat, they draw the nutrients with their fingerlike projections, but if the villi are damaged or flattened, which is what happens from inflammation, the food just cruises by and ends in your colon. If the food is lacking fiber, there is nothing to sweep that toxic waste through the colon, so the food sits there, rotting, creating everything from constipation and weight gain to weakened immune system and depression. That's when everything goes south: The colon wall begins to absorb the toxins created by rotting food and releasing them into the bloodstream as free radicals that roam your body seeking healthy cells to invade. You can probably finish this paragraph yourself . . . the end result is not pretty.

Thankfully, a number of mainstream medical doctors, such as Dr. Alejandro Junger, Dr. Gerard Mullin, and Dr. David Perlmutter, have jumped on the gut-cleaning bandwagon, educating us about the importance of caring for our gut, good and bad bacteria, and explaining in detail the role healthy digestion plays in our well-being. Our digestive system even has a new term, "second brain," which is often used in the media. I say, it's about time. My dream is to see every doctor, including pediatricians, ask all patients about their diet and lifestyle, and guide us to respect our body without submitting it to external aggressions that knock us out of balance. And I think a time will come in the very near future when we begin to celebrate our lower body's achievements, and not feel ashamed or apologetic.

Why Do We Get Sick?

Now that you are up to speed on the importance of healthy digestion and believe that nurturing your gut is as important as nurturing your soul, it will be no surprise to you that sickness comes when our immune system is weakened. If you take the time to heal the gut, which houses 90 percent of our immune system, you are on your way to giving your body's fighter cells the green light to destroy and eliminate any intruders, whether it's cancer cells or a flu virus.

Many of us grow up thinking illness is a part of life, an inevitable, natural thing. The allergies, the headaches, the colds, the flu, the fatigue, even aging—all that seems normal. But just because it's so common in our society, that doesn't make it normal. We mistake being able to function with being vibrant and healthy. *Healthy* doesn't mean being able to just go through our daily routines; *healthy* means functioning at our highest level.

But why do we get sick? Can we do anything to avoid sickness? The answer is a resounding yes! Would you believe me if I told you that we make ourselves sick by making bad choices? And get healthy and stay healthy by making good ones? Does that sound too simple? Well, it *is* simple!

We are not told that *we* have the power to make profound choices about our health. That's why, when we get sick, we look to something outside of ourselves to explain why we are sick. Health is not something that happens *to* us! You don't get a cold because somebody was coughing and sneezing near you at work; you get a cold because your immune system is low (you stayed up late, drank too much wine, worked too much, etc.) and couldn't fight for you. We invite illness with our poor choices.

POTTY TALK

Not to get too anal, but did you know that sitting on the toilet is bad for your health? I bet you've never heard that. Unless you watch *Shark Tank,* the popular TV show where wealthy entrepreneurs invest in small businesses, and saw Lori Greiner putting her money into Squatty Potty, a plastic stool that wraps around your commode and helps you poop. I suggest you all go out and buy yourself one.

Trust me when I tell you that squatting is the new sitting. (There is actually science to that!) Various studies show that we are more efficient at eliminating if we squat, that squatting is far more natural and puts less pressure on our tush, helps with constipation, protects us from hemorrhoids and bowel diseases, plus ensures a healthy colon. Stanford University's Pelvic Floor Clinic even requires patients with colon issues to squat and not sit on the toilet.

Our body consists of trillions of cells and our immune system depends on their functioning well. Of course, it's almost an impossible task to keep all the cells functioning perfectly and the challenge is to have minimum malfunction. Our body is so incredible: We produce more than 10 million new cells every second as we constantly rebuild our tissues. So, if we make even a small change in how we eat, our new cells will be built stronger. You can't argue with the fact that we have to build new cells with proper materials, just like when you are building a house! Because if we replace sick cells with sick cells, we will never recover.

One of the best places to start on the road to wellness and optimum health is in your kitchen. Choosing organic produce for your soups, salads, and other recipes is not optional. Sometimes it costs a little more, but if you think about your health as the most important investment, why not spend a little more? If you get sick, you don't think twice about paying whatever to buy your doctor's prescription. So why, then, is your paying more for organic food any different?

But wellness is not all about nutrition. It's also about your emotions and spirit, your lifestyle, the way you move your body, your genetics, and what you choose to do about them. I'm a big believer that if you are passionate about living your healthiest life, you will stop what you are doing that made you sick and start new habits that will heal you. I did. And guess what? A miracle happened. I proved to my doctors that the genetic tests that predicted the return of cancer within seventeen months were wrong . . . and all I had to do is change.

What Should I Eat?

We all want a lean and sexy body, and we've been taught to count calories so we can achieve our goals. Calories in, calories out, right? Wrong! I intentionally don't have a caloric panel of the Soupelina soups because I think counting calories is a ridiculous waste of time. Instead, we need to start counting nutrients! Because a 300-calorie bowl of soup, packed with antioxidant veggies and herbs, contributes to a healthy body, while a 100-calorie bag of candy, with no nutrients and only a bunch of sugar and processed junk, only contributes to illness and does absolutely nothing for your health.

Promise me that from now on you will never count calories again. And when you prepare your meals, you will count the goodness of the organic ingredients and will do everything to include as many superfoods as you can in each bowl or plate. You need to make sure that your food is free of toxins and filled with nutrients that support your body's natural ability to detoxify.

You need to know what's in your food, where your food came from, and whether your food has been altered from its natural state. "But how do I know what's good for me?" you ask. We are bombarded with so much conflicting information, articles, and opinions on food and nutrition that it's fair to say we live in the food information overload age.

Not a month goes by that a food formerly praised by nutritionists is all of a sudden vilified by scientists. One moment, soy is a miracle food; the next, soy is terrible for you. Even kale, touted as the greatest superfood on earth, was recently knocked off its pedestal. No wonder we begin to rebel: Who has the time to keep track of it all? Ironically, modern medicine is now telling us that our food choices can prevent disease and aging. How do we cut through the noise and know what we can and what we shouldn't eat?

After six years researching and studying this question to help myself, I arrived at something I not only believe in completely, I live it. I know that my food is healing and good for my body if:

+ My food makes me healthy.

+ My food makes me feel light and energetic.

+ My food increases my well-being.

+ My food invigorates my senses.

+ My food keeps me looking young and prevents aging.

I know my body so well now that I can immediately tell whether what I ate was good for me. I eat my food freshly prepared; I don't like frozen, microwaved, and canned foods; I also almost never eat leftovers. I believe the fresher the food, the more life force it has, and that provides me with energy and good health.

Buying organic is super important! I cannot stress that enough. Organic means that your food was grown without chemical fertilizers and pesticides, artificial ripening agents, preservatives, genetic modifications, and radiation, all potentially cancer-causing. So many fruits and veggies can be a major cancer risk if not bought organic. The Environmental Working Group (ewg.org) found that almost all (up to 98%) of all conventional produce is contaminated with cancer-causing pesticides.

Sugar, milk, white flour, and certain oils can all be quietly contributing to toxicity, and combined with stress, lack of exercise, environmental factors, and modern life, are the ingredients for all kinds of chronic conditions, including cancer.

Although we are led to believe that it's our genes or environmental factors that cause us to get sick, it's most likely our lifestyle. "Wait, that sounds like crap," you are probably thinking, because you know all these people who eat junk, smoke, drink, and never get cancer. And then you heard about that vegetarian friend of a friend, who was a runner and made all the right choices and got cancer. How does it work? Are there actually cancer-causing foods that can harm you even when you think you are eating healthy? Apparently so!

Making the case against meat and poultry is easy. The World Health Organization (WHO) now classifies processed meats as "carcinogenic to humans" and warns that unprocessed red meat may also be carcinogenic. And who hasn't seen the YouTube videos about the treatment of animals, the hormones and antibiotics they are injected with, the way the animals are killed, the way the meat is handled, and so on. I won't go there. But there are a few other foods I do want to talk about.

Skip Milk!

But milk? It's supposed to be great for us, for our bones, teeth, health. To this day, I find it hard convincing people that milk and other dairy are not good for us. So, I recommend they read *The China Study* by T. Colin Campbell, a respected Cornell University scientist and pioneer in the investigation of the diet-cancer link. The book was my "aha" moment because it had all the scientific proof that the food we eat directly contributes to our health, and that even cancer cells can be turned off by choosing plant-based nutrition. It's wonderful to see other scientists joining the plant-based chorus and educating us on why it should be "Skip Milk!" and not "Got Milk?" Milk isn't sexy, it's not healthy, and it doesn't help you grow strong bones. If you are really into the white liquid, choose hemp, rice or almond milks. And for Soupelina's sake, don't add any cream to your nutritious soups.

Stop Sugarcoating!

You've heard that sugar feeds cancer cells. Well, it does. Cancer cells metabolize sugars to thrive. This is one thing I don't understand: Why do we add sugar to food? Real food doesn't need it, but I guess without sugar we would be able to taste all the chemicals in those processed boxed goods. I was shocked to learn how many foods contain massive amounts of sugar. Salad dressings, juices, protein bars, breads, cereals, designer waters, even most soups are all loaded with sugar, and I'm not even mentioning chocolate, soft drinks, desserts, and snacks. The list goes on.

There's been so much sugar talk lately that unless you live under a rock, you've heard at least some of it. I will just say that sugar equals chaos in your body and throws you out of balance almost immediately. All sugar calories are empty calories, with zero nutrients; you just promised me to start counting your nutrients, didn't you? Sugar is so dodgy, it's actually an antinutrient!

It drains nutrients from your body, stripping you of calcium, making your bones weaker, and contributing to osteoporosis. Sugar damages the cells of your immune system and creates susceptibility to colds, flu, and more serious diseases. You are sweet enough; you don't need to sugarcoat your food. Learn to enjoy it in its natural form.

Quit White Flour!

I admit, it's tasty. So tasty, in fact, that if I have a slice of bread, I end up eating the entire loaf. But once I realized that white flour can lead to disease, quitting it was worth the effort. A plate of pasta with veggies is not a good meal. Noodles in your soup are not a good choice, either. Whole grains (such as brown rice, buckwheat, amaranth, millet, and teff), and beans (think lentils and favas) are much better for you. And there are so many nutritious flours now, made from whole foods, such as chickpeas or almonds. They are real foods, not their make-believe cousins. White flour has a high glycemic index, which means it raises blood sugar levels and can promote rapid cancer cell growth.

Say No to GMOs!

Isn't it funny how something that is supposedly created to do good ends up being evil? We are told that GMOs (genetically modified organisms) were developed to help with malnutrition and world hunger, but the opposite happened. Studies have shown that both GMOs and the chemicals used to grow them cause rapid tumor growth. Most of the US corn and soy crops are genetically modified, and genetically modified ingredients are in some 70 percent of processed foods! So, why tempt fate and eat this crap, when you can enjoy whole organic foods? (And if you're especially into corn on the cob or edamame, be sure to only buy certified organic.)

Choose Your Oils!

The good news is that the US Food and Drug Administration (FDA) recently banned partially hydrogenated oils (PHOs) and gave manufacturers three years to phase them out. But did you know that most oils on your supermarket shelves are processed and toxic? (Not just bottled oils; remember

Soupelina

that they are also in the salad dressings, baked goods, and canned and boxed foods.) Many oils are created through chemical extraction methods, making them detrimental to your health. Even cold-pressed oils are too often refined with toxic chemicals and exposed to high temperatures when they are being bleached, making them toxic. When cooking, choose high-quality extra-virgin olive oil, coconut oil, and sesame oil. Olive oil does not do well in high heat, so reserve it as a base for your herbal oils to top the soups.

· · ·

The rest of the list is pretty much self-explanatory. There is no room for any of these foods in your new healthy kitchen:

+ DIET AND SOFT DRINKS are loaded with sugar or artificial sweeteners, food chemicals, and colorings. It's like drinking a slow suicide potion. Almost every ingredient in colas has been linked to cancer. Stop drinking them immediately. A UCLA study also found a direct link between soft drinks and obesity.

+ CANNED FOODS, especially soups, are off limits! No matter how pretty the packaging, multiple studies and reports reveal a direct link between BPA-lined cans and cancers, especially breast cancer. BPA compound mimics estrogen hormones that can disrupt your endocrine system.

+ POTATO CHIPS AND FRENCH FRIES, two of America's favorite foods are full of trans fats, sodium, artificial flavors and colors. The grossest thing is that the high temperatures used to cook the chips and fries cause the formation of acrylamide, a carcinogenic substance also found in cigarettes.

+ MICROWAVE POPCORN. The bags that house the kernels are lined with all kinds of chemicals, linked to causing infertility and a number of cancers.

The Power of Ayurveda, Chinese Medicine, Homeopathy, and Folk Remedies

What did people know centuries ago that we still don't? Why are we seeing the resurgence in the ancient healing medicines now, when our so-called unprecedented medical advances have been so lauded? And why is ancient medicine called "alternative"?

When I spoke with doctors of Chinese and Ayurvedic medicine, homeopaths, integrative, and conventional physicians, the consensus seems to be that when it comes to chronic conditions and cancer, the system isn't working. Modern medicine is a study of disease and doctors are taught in school how to treat disease, not how to prevent it and maintain their patients' wellness. Everyone agrees that treating symptoms is important, but what really matters in achieving optimum health is taking responsibility in your own healing.

Studies support this, showing that more than one-third of Americans are looking to alternative medicine for answers, creating a growing field of Integrative Medicine. With all the different approaches on the table, how do you know what's right for you?

There is a lot to digest here, but look at different healing modalities as ingredients in your health. You wouldn't want to just eat kale all year long. Why settle on the conventional approach alone? Sample, see what works for you, and you might be surprised that in the process you will feel healthier, happier, and certainly more balanced.

Ayurveda

More and more people are looking to Ayurveda (which translates from Sanskrit as "science of life") to heal what ails them. Despite being more than five thousand years old and the oldest health-care system in the world, Ayurveda is experiencing a renaissance in the West. What's behind the revival, practitioners say, is that Ayurveda offers wisdom to help people stay vital and healthy, rather than just receive occasional treatments. Ayurveda focuses on prevention and natural healing, and is based on the principles of your body's constitution, personal experience, and the harmonious relationship with food.

At the heart of Ayurveda is the concept of the three doshas, or the three different types of human constitution, acquired at birth, which remain constant through life. Vata, Pitta, and Kapha vital energies make up every one of us, and when they are in harmony, the result is optimal health.

According to Ayurveda, the imbalance of your vital energies leads to the development of disease. If the oldest medicine in the world believes that, I'm on board! I actually think it's more relevant today than it was many years ago.

Soupelina

Soup Is the Key

with Martha Soffer, Ayurvedic therapist and Ayurvedic chef

Originally from Colombia, Martha Soffer is an internationally acclaimed Ayurveda Panchakarma expert, Ayurvedic chef, herbal rasayanist, and master Ayurvedic pulse diagnostician. She studied the ancient medicine at the Maharishi University, and trained in India and also at the American University of Complementary Medicine.

I met Martha three years after my diagnosis. I was looking for ways to find balance. People whose lives she's transformed recommended her to me.

EF: How do you explain Ayurveda to those who have never heard about it before?

MS: The cornerstone of Ayurveda is the focus on food and lifestyle, and instead of leaving my clinic with a prescription for pills, you are most likely to leave with a recipe or two. I love to prescribe soups! Soups are easy to digest: They are warming, which increases the absorption of nutrients, making soups especially nourishing. In general, soups balance our Vata, as soups are soothing and calming. Depending on the ingredients, any fresh and nourishing soup can balance any of our doshas: Coconut, cilantro, and cucumber, for example, are very cooling for overheated Pitta; radish, celery, and leafy greens, for example, are stimulating to an overtired or mucusy Kapha.

EF: Why cleanse with soups, not juices?

MS: Juices, while healthy and full of good vitamins and nutrients, aggravate Vata because they make the digestion cold, which requires the system to work harder. Soups give you more digestible nutrients, and create more satiety—you feel nourished, and you are. Soups, especially soups like dhal, are filled with protein, and you can live on them for as long as you like!

EF: What happens in your body when you cleanse with Ayurvedic soups?

MS: Because the body relaxes with the ease of nutritious and easy-to-digest soups, all the organs are given a little time off, as it were, and organs like the liver and kidney can more easily dispose of toxins. The entire system gets a break, and can do its own work of self-repair and renewal. In general, the

WHAT DOSHA AM I?

The good news is that you don't have to travel to India to find your dosha. Simply locate a certified Ayurvedic practitioner in your area who can help you. There are many online quizzes that provide basic guidelines, but I found that they are not always accurate; when I took them, I got varying results that left me even more confused. The most precise determination comes from a practitioner who is trained to diagnose your dosha through pulse reading and other diagnostic tools, such as looking at your eyes and tongue. That said, here are the basic guidelines to help you identify your constitutional nature.

First off, every single one of us contains the dynamic forces of all three doshas—Vata, Pitta, and Kapha—but usually one or two dominates. The difference is also the degree to which these doshas interact within each type.

+ Vata

Vata governs all movements and motion; it is the most powerful of the doshas and the strongest to create disease. Vata individuals are generally slender, creative, alert, restless, and fast-talking; have a fun personality, changeable moods, quick to learn and also quick to forget; have a tendency toward cold feet and hands, don't like cold climates. Vata body types are prone to constipation, seldom perspire, and sleep lightly; they are high energy but also tire easily and tend to overexert themselves. When in balance, Vata people are most creative, full of joy and enthusiasm. Out of balance, they are fearful, anxious, and tend to act on impulse. Vata types are susceptible to nerve disorders, digestive issues, insomnia, and arthritis.

warming of the system helps everything that shouldn't be in you melt away. Even fat, moving out of your body, will be more easily released.

EF: Does it matter what ingredients and spices to include?

MS: Absolutely! Mung bean dhal is balancing for all three doshas, but every ingredient affects the doshas—just think how you start sweating after a spicy curry, or how refreshed you feel after a cucumber soup! It's good to know what dosha feels out of balance, and you can find ingredients (even by look-

Soupelina

+ Pitta

Pitta governs heat, temperature, and all transformations. Pitta individuals have a strong, well-built physique and sharp mind; they are assertive, competitive, self-confident, and have great entrepreneurial spirit; they are passionate and enjoy challenges, but also prone to impatience, anger, and temper tantrums. Pitta body types perspire a lot and their sweat has a strong odor; when under stress, they can be gluttonous, irritated, and angry. When in balance, Pitta people are content and brilliant leaders. Out of balance, they are arrogant, irritable, and even angry. Pitta types are susceptible to ulcers, heartburn, high blood pressure, acne and other skin conditions, anemia, and inflammation.

+ Kapha

Kapha is governed by nourishment; it's responsible for growth, supplies water to all the body parts, and maintains the immune system. Kapha individuals generally tend to carry extra weight; they are slow-paced, easygoing, compassionate, loving, and nonjudgmental in nature; they speak slower and have a great long-term memory. Kaphas are gentle, stable, grounded, not easy to upset, but tend to be possessive and hold on to things. When in balance, Kapha people are loving and calm. Out of balance, they are insecure and envious. Kapha types suffer from colds, congestion, sinus headaches, asthma, and allergies; they gain weight, can have benign tumors, and are prone to diabetes.

ing online) that can work to rebalance that dosha (ingredients to cool, calm, and stimulate your physiology). Food truly is medicine, and we can feel its effects after a single meal.

EF: I'm fascinated by "plant power." Can you increase or decrease this power with veggies, herbs, and spices?

MS: Every plant contains some medicinal value. Sometimes the skin of a plant will contain an entirely different medicinal value than the meat of the plant, like the skin of the mung bean, for example, which is used to detoxify the blood and remove poison. Plant power also has to do with seasons—our bodies move with the seasons, and the food we favor should follow the same, natural, seasonal pattern. Ayurveda helps us understand our connection to the seasons, to the land, to food—as we are all part of one, moving natural system. The stronger our relationship with our natural environment, the better chance we have of having better health.

EF: What conditions can Ayurveda treat?

MS: Ayurveda treats the root of our problems—specifically and generally. In Western medicine, if you show your doctor a rash, he might prescribe a steroid cream to rub on the rash. This is known as "coming down on the symptom" to eradicate it. And that might be a very effective eradication. In Ayurveda, the Ayurvedic doctor finds the underlying imbalance that has, much later in the physiological process, given rise to the symptom, in this case, the rash. By working to bring the underlying imbalance back in good order, not only does the symptom naturally disappear, so do the whole range of related symptoms, either manifest or manifesting, that stem from that same imbalance. Ayurveda doesn't treat the leaf, it treats the root. Because of this, Ayurveda treats the widest range of conditions, from skin and weight issues, to serious neurological conditions. Finally, Ayurveda isn't an alternative system of health, it's really a complementary one—many Western doctors choose Ayurveda to supplement their own health, and many doctors send their patients to me to either detoxify after serious courses of medicine, or because they've run up against a wall.

Chinese Medicine

Just as Ayurveda is about doshas, Traditional Chinese Medicine (TCM) is about yin and yang. Yin and yang are both energies, the opposite forces of nature, and balancing them is important in achieving optimum health. Yang is warm, yin is cold, and they depend on each other to keep our body in balance.

While not everyone knows about yin and yang when it comes to medicine, most of you have heard of acupuncture, the insertion of hair-thin needles into particular places (called points) of your body to access the chi (energy) that is blocked or not flowing right. Acupuncture has certainly gone mainstream in the past decade. Many Western doctors have embraced it, even sending their patients to acupuncturists for specific conditions. Acupuncture, along with Chinese herbal medicine, is a part of TCM, and in tandem sees disease in terms of patterns of disharmony. Energy is believed to flow through channels called meridians, through which a disease can be diagnosed, treated, and prevented. Food is important in Chinese medicine; its energetic and therapeutic properties are vital in strengthening our organ systems and sustaining balance between energies and organs.

Healing Wisdom

with Dr. Mao Shing Ni, Doctor of Traditional Chinese Medicine, L.Ac., D.O.M., Ph.D., Dipl. C.H., ABAAP, authority in antiaging

My surgeon, Dr. Kristi Funk, introduced me to Dr. Mao Shing Ni, or Dr. Mao, the foremost expert on Traditional Chinese Medicine, at the very beginning of my healing journey. Within moments on my very first visit, he immediately knew how to treat me. A thirty-eighth-generation herbalist, Dr. Mao used herb potions he would assemble each time along with the acupuncture to get my body in harmony. He also taught me about the power of food, necessity of detoxing, Qigong, and being kind to myself.

EF: When I first came to you in 2009, you told me that my cancer "wasn't physical," and that set me on a course of figuring out what I can do to heal myself. What do you see when people come to you with diagnoses like cancer and other chronic conditions?

MN: Cancer is characterized by cells' growing abnormally, and the answer we seek is why. In Chinese medicine it has long been recognized that cancer is a result of blockage of energy, blood, toxins, and negative emotions.

EF: How does Chinese medicine help people heal?

MN: Chinese medicine is a medical system focused on the whole person, which includes their mind, spirit, and body as well as the disease. It seeks to restore the person's innate ability to heal his or her self through acupuncture, which "reprograms" the body's healing system, herbal/nutritional therapies that support the healing process, and meditation/mind-body exercise to encourage patient participation.

EF: I grew up on soups but I never thought of soups as healing until I met you. You introduced that concept to me. Why are soups so powerful in healing?

MN: Soups make most of the nutrients from food that's being cooked easily assimilated for the body. Soups make nutrients and active ingredients easy to digest and absorb. Healthy soups also satiate without the additional calories. Soups are a good way for patients who want to cleanse, lose weight, and generally wanting to start on a healthy eating regimen. Soups have been enjoyed by all cultures from around the world.

The earliest medical canon in the world—the Yellow Emperor's Classic on Medicine—contained formulas and recipes for soups made from herbs, vegetables, like a dandelion fennel soup for cleansing. Early in its history, Chinese medicine developed the science of food healing by discovering and applying healing properties of each food for prevention and disease treatment.

EF: How does nutrition and lifestyle affect our health?

MN: Nutrition is most fundamental to health and healing and is considered the first line of prevention and healing for disease in Chinese medicine. I've seen many patients profoundly change their health and lives through changing their diet. For example, one heart disease patient vastly lowered his bad LDL cholesterol from over 230 to less than 100 by changing to a plant-based diet. Another patient with diabetes was able to stop his medication after cutting out fats, refined carbohydrates, and sugar and increased his intake of vegetables and lean proteins like fish and losing about 25 pounds. A third patient with crippling arthritis became pain-free and off four medications after being on an anti-inflammatory diet consisting of vegetables and juices and broth made of vegetables.

EF: Why is it important to integrate traditional approach (Western medicine) with alternative (Eastern medicine) when it comes to disease?

MN: Western medicine excels in "killing" disease, while Eastern medicine's strength is in supporting and fortifying the body's vitality and functions. With integration, a cancer patient can expect to have better quality of life and higher survival rate.

Soupelina

Homeopathy and Naturopathy

Homeopathic and naturopathic medicine are complementary health-care modalities that treat a person as a whole or holistically. Doctors of homeopathy and naturopathy believe that with proper attention our body is capable of healing itself without harsh invasive treatments. The complete and holistic system of healing was developed in the 1700s by a German physician, Samuel Hahnemann. He was disillusioned by the treatments of the time and was one of the first to advocate proper hygiene, good diet, fresh air, and higher standards of living. Homeopathy was practiced by many American doctors in the 1800s, but then was pushed out of the medical system when the American Medical Association was formed. Interestingly, homeopathy is now experiencing resurgence in popularity as people search for safe, holistic treatments to replace the toxic drugs their doctors prescribe.

Getting to the Root Cause

with Dr. Gez Agolli, ND, Ph.D.

I met Dr. Gez Agolli when a friend introduced me to his Progressive Medical Center in Atlanta, Georgia, an impressive, one-of-a-kind clinic with an integrative, 360-degree approach to health: a new paradigm for wellness that combines holistic medicine—treating the whole person, not just the physical body—with state-of-the-art diagnostic tools. Dr. Agolli taught me to integrate my therapies and do my own research. I have since visited Progressive several times and always consult with Dr. Agolli when my daughters or I feel out of balance or are in need of a tune-up.

EF: Let's talk about your approach in treating people.

GA: Getting to the root cause of an illness is the key. It's most important to understand where the disease came from in the first place. As a naturopath with training in homeopathy, I utilize all aspects of medicine to integrate traditional, osteopathic, naturopathic, Ayurvedic, Oriental, and homeopathic modalities. What I practice is healing-oriented medicine that treats the whole person (body, mind, and spirit), including all aspects of lifestyle. It emphasizes the therapeutic relationship and makes use of all appropriate therapies, both conventional and alternative. Naturopathic physicians prescribe multiple treatment approaches, like supplements, herbs and dietary adjustments. Our body has an innate ability to heal itself if we give it what it needs, such as proper rest, an anti-inflammatory diet, vitamins, and minerals. Strengthening the immune system is important, first by clearing your body of toxins, followed by a healthy, mainly plant-based diet, packed with green veggies, soups, no dairy, very lean meat, frequent exercise, reduced stress, and noninvasive therapies.

EF: We are used to blood and urine testing when we go to a doctor; I was impressed with all the other tests I did at your clinic.

GA: Our main goal is to understand the history of the patient; that's why, besides blood work and urine, we collect saliva, stool, and hair. We also spend time discussing a patient's lifestyle, nutrition, and habits. All this helps us in determining their current immune system status. We take your entire self into consideration—your mind, body, and spirit—so illnesses caused by stress, autoimmune factors, and chronic illness are very well understood.

EF: How do natural therapies help build the immune system?

GA: Our immune system is quite complex. We actually have two immune systems: humoral (outside the cell) and cellular (inside the cell). The humoral system has a memory; the cell does not and will not attack. Because our immune system is the first line of defense against external invaders, such as viruses, bacteria, parasites, mycoplasma, and other co-infections that wreak havoc on the human body, nutrition and natural therapies are vital to a well-functioning immune system. The immune system has evolved in humans to protect us from these opportunistic pathogenic microorganisms and cancer. Cells and organs of the immune system are derived from bone marrow and the thymus gland as primary organs, and secondary organs are lymph nodes, spleen, and mucosal lymphoid tissue (MALT). Therefore, proper nutrition, such as minerals, vitamins, essential amino acids, and essential fatty acids, are vital to enhance and build the immune system. A strong healthy immune system is a strong, healthy you!

EF: We know that proper nutrition is important, but people are still reluctant to believe that food can heal.

GA: Food is medicine. Hippocrates, the father of modern medicine, stated centuries ago, "Let your medicine be your food and your food be your medicine!" Bottom line is, food is vital to your health. And nutritious soup is especially nourishing to the body and the soul when it's created properly, because soup can enhance the absorption of minerals and vitamins due to the preparation process.

EF: Juice cleansing has been really popular in the past few years and we are just beginning to see the medicinal benefits of cleansing with soups. So, is it juicing or souping when it comes to cleansing?

GA: I prefer to cleanse with soups and broths instead of juices, because soups and broths during cleansing are more filling and are lower on glycemic index, which balances out the blood sugar and avoids a candida (yeast) flare-up. Most of us are sensitive to high-sugar foods and most juice fasts will affect your pancreas and could eventually lead to insulin resistance, if not monitored properly. You will not have this issue with wholesome soups. Also soups are much more satisfying and soothing during a cleanse.

EF: How does our body eliminate toxins when we eat soups?

GA: Your body will gently eliminate toxins from organs and cells and will allow the body to heal itself and get back into balance. You will enhance your metabolism and lose unwanted pounds lodged as unhealthy adipose tissue affecting your overall health and well-being.

EF: What are the best anti-inflammatory soup ingredients?

GA: Turmeric, ginger, garlic, onions, olive oil, beets, dark green leafy vegetables, tomatoes, and peppers. If you are feeling out of balance, my prescription would be *Soupelina's* Veggie Healing Broth (page 179) with my spices (see page 20) and onion. Works like a charm!

SPICE IT UP WITH ELEVEN HEAVEN, DR. AGOLLI'S HEALTHY SPICE MIX.

2 tablespoons smoked paprika

1 tablespoon garlic powder

1 tablespoon dried oregano

1 tablespoon onion powder

1 tablespoon dried basil

2 teaspoons dried thyme

1 ½ teaspoons freshly ground black pepper

1 ½ teaspoons fine-grain sea salt

1 teaspoon freshly ground white pepper (optional)

1 teaspoon cayenne pepper

½ teaspoon ground turmeric

FOLK REMEDIES

Since the beginning of times, every culture has had its own ways of healing diseases. Whether it was local plants, customs, or beliefs, the age-old wisdom got passed on from generation to generation. A return to old ways has been very trendy lately, mostly because with all the technological advances, we have forgotten how to take care of ourselves. We've become so dependent on doctors, drugs, and store-bought food that most of us don't even know our own body.

And with greater responsibility placed on us to stay healthy and prevent illness, and greater costs of health care, the popularity of folk or home remedies is no joke. They work.

I grew up with compresses, poultices, and baths to help with minor ailments when I was a kid. Tea bags for conjunctivitis, walnut bark for toothache, baked onions for cysts, mustard baths for sore throat, baking soda for indigestion . . . I barely went to doctors unless things were more serious.

I believe in the power of plants and ancient traditions. Folk remedies are certainly not a substitute for medical care, but they reduce the number of doctor's visits, and most important, they are powerful in preventing serious chronic conditions. So, don't laugh them off but instead, talk to your mom or grandma, who I'm sure has a few up her sleeve. There are also hundreds of books with remedies for most common health issues, such as insect bites, back pain, fever, and even ear infections that can be safely treated at home. I often refer to the Mayo Clinic's *Book of Home Remedies* or National Geographic's *The People Pharmacy* books.

3

DIVING IN

I know you can't wait to start souping. You might have even skipped the first two chapters and looked through recipes because you are so ready. Yay, you!

But now you are back because you have questions: Do I need any special tools? Where do I get my ingredients—some of them sound so foreign!? Why can't I use fruits and nuts in my soups? Aren't they supposed to be good for me? Let's give it a whirl and get into the nitty-gritty of setting up your kitchen and your new life.

FIRST THINGS FIRST

You are about to embark on a souping adventure and you have to be ready. Do you have all your ducks in a row? Let me show you how.

SET A GOAL. Decide what you can handle, but I suggest you challenge yourself. Go outside your comfort zone and really do it! Set a date, cancel all the dinner plans, and commit. I know you want to fit into those skinny jeans, but think health first, and don't jump into a cleanse if your friend is having a birthday party and you know you're going to want to snack and drink along with everyone else.

SHARE THE LOVE. It's harder to make changes alone, and if you can get a partner, spouse, lover, friend or even the kids on board, you will have someone close to you to lean on. If that's not an option, don't fret; I will show you how you can fill your days cleansing without feeling as if you are missing out.

MAKE IT AN EXPERIENCE. The idea of cleansing may be a little intimidating, but try to think of it as an adventure and an opportunity for new experiences. Schedule your farmers market shopping days, explore a new side of town with little ethnic stores you've never been to, go on a hike, try meditation . . . you know what I mean.

GET THE JUNK OUT. Go through your kitchen, clear the pantry, empty the fridge, and fill them with fresh organic produce, organic spices and herbs, and legumes.

Set your intentions, and you are ready to roll. Oops, I meant, ready to soup!

The Tools

It's like soup was meant for us folks who want to change our health and our lives on our own terms. Soup is forgiving, relatively easy to cook, and doesn't require many specialized pieces of equipment. I bet you already have plenty of pots, skillets, and baking sheets in your kitchen. But to be a super soup-er, you do need a few things that will make your life easier and soups tastier.

Here is my list of souping helpers.

POTS are at the top of the soup chain. Buy the wrong pot and the soup will not taste good; it's that simple. Cooking soups is a labor of love; you want to make sure that your pot has a heavy bottom so your veggies don't scorch and stick. And nonstick and Teflon cookware have no room in your new healthy soup-er kitchen. Nonsticks have turned that love into a health hazard because of the toxic chemicals these pots are made with.

I love copper pots because of the way they distribute heat; stainless-steel ones are great, too. They make your kitchen look professional, but choose pieces that have an aluminum or copper base. A 6-quart soup pot is a good size for most soups, and if you really get into it, consider buying a larger 10- to 12-quart stockpot for broths.

SKILLET is essential for sautéing. If you have a nonstick one, toss it. I use only my heavy, cast-iron skillet that has been loved and seasoned, and makes even a simple onion taste scrumptious. Cast-iron cookware has been around for hundreds of years and there's a reason it's still around today. It's that good.

VITAMIX is a must for your soup kitchen. You just gotta have it! This superpowered blender is a game changer and a lifesaver. How else would you be able to puree your hot and cold soups? I use mine several times per day and even travel with it. Vitamix is pricey but so worth it and will last you forever. I actually looked into other high-speed blenders to recommend and none can compete with Vitamix. Blendtec is a close second. An immersion blender lets you blend your soup in the pot and saves a step or two, but I'm not a big fan of the consistency, especially when it comes to al dente veggies.

PEELER A good one is not so easy to find. I've gone through at least a dozen and the one I love the most I bought in a tiny Asian store. Look for an easy-to-hold, comfortable handle and a sharp but not serrated blade.

SHARP KNIVES are the backbone of any kitchen. I have many knives, but I seem to gravitate toward ceramic knives. I find them easier, lighter, and more sanitary. Let me explain. Ceramic knives are not very porous and that keeps the blade from transferring odors from garlic to tomato, for example.

It won't transfer the spiciness, either. They don't rust and they stay sharp, plus if it ever needs sharpening, the manufacturer sharpens it for free. What a deal! I work with a chef's knife, a small paring knife, and a serrated knife.

GARLIC MINCER is one of my favorites and most-used tools besides Vitamix. I don't go anywhere without it, probably because I adore garlic! Just as with the peeler, it's not easy to find the tool that does the job and also lasts. So many break within days of using. The one that lasted me the longest I bought at a market in Barcelona. Currently, I'm having a great experience with the Ikea mincer.

CUTTING BOARDS get a lot of use, so get several. Have a large one for big leafy veggies and squashes, and a smaller one for tomatoes, onions, avocados, and herbs. I prefer wooden and bamboo boards—they feel earthy and real to me—instead of slippery plastic ones, which can also breed bacteria.

BAKING SHEETS OR A BAKING PAN are the miracle tools that help transform squashes, carrots, sweet potatoes, or beets into golden bites of veggie caramel. Make sure your baking sheet is metal with low sides so the oven heat can envelope the veggies from three sides. For easy cleanup, line it with foil or parchment paper.

WOODEN AND SILICONE SPOONS are the best for sautéing, mixing, and scooping the soup. I have a large collection of flat, square wooden spoons; I cannot live without them! Silicone spoons and spatulas endure high temperatures and are ideal for scraping all the goodness out of the Vitamix when the blending is done.

MEASURING CUPS AND SPOONS are probably already in your kitchen and will make your life easier, especially if you are just starting out.

VEGGIE BRUSH is a great addition to your healthy kitchen. Naturally, I prefer the wooden brush with both soft and firm bristles.

LADLES. Picking the right one is like picking a partner! Seriously, ladles are a big deal, but I know many well-equipped kitchens that don't have one.

My beloved All-Clad ladle that my daughters gave me is not only a perfect soup companion, but also a lucky charm (Madeline and Isabelle had "Soupelina" engraved on mine).

SCALE is optional but can be useful for beginners and those who like to be very careful with proportions. If you spring for one, make sure it measures metric as well.

JARS are perfect for storing soup in the fridge and even carrying soups around. They are sturdy, dishwasher-safe, and don't retain flavors. You can eat from them as well, plus they look pretty!

MUSIC to cook to. Yup, that's a necessity! My music selection is seasonal, just like my veggies. In the fall, I go for Melody Gardot and my daughter Madeline; in the winter, I love Ella Fitzgerald and Nat King Cole; spring is my Lana Del Rey time; and summer is for Steve Tyrell. Choose the music that speaks to you and helps you create in the kitchen. There is nothing like good food + good music together.

THE FIRST BEST INGREDIENT: WATER

Water is a really important part of souping. It must be good. Because if it isn't, what's the point of a healing soup? The soup's delicate flavors can be completely ruined by chlorinated water, not to mention all the chemical deposits that are downright toxic for both cooking and washing your veggies. You may want to use filtered water, purified water, or spring water. And if you are in the middle of cancer treatments, a food-grade hydrogen peroxide soak is a good idea for making sure your veggies are extra clean.

When you start cooking, you will see that I love using water and not broth in my veggie soups. I love my wonderful veggies to cook in their own juices and keep the flavors intact without introducing additional veggie broth flavorings. I find vegetable stock brings a more assertive flavor to soups. Besides, for me, broth is a separate meal, not a cooking addition to the soups.

Soupelina

The Ingredients

Until I launched Soupelina in February 2013, bland soups from the grocery stores and canned soups made from unpronounceable ingredients were the only options. Even upscale restaurant soups had dairy, nuts, soy, and other allergens, and some even had sugar, making soups a relatively unhealthy and uninspiring choice. I decided to change that by introducing soups that were as pure as the organic, locally sourced seasonal ingredients I use to cook them. As a journalist, I also set out to educate people on the importance of eating soups that are made by slowly cooking them and allowing veggies to release their nutrients, thus aiding and healing the digestive system.

You already know that food is medicine, but soups take it up a notch. Because it's not just veggies, but also herbs and spices and their particular combination that have the medicinal value. To make a healing soup you have to handpick your ingredients, using the freshest veggies, rather than last week's sad produce buried in your fridge crisper.

The flavor of your soup and the holistic idea of your soup should resonate with you long after you have eaten it. Soup is not just about the squash or the fennel, it's what that squash and fennel represent. It's so much larger than a bowl of soup.

Because of this, in this book you won't see any traditional soups you are used to. No tomato-basil, chowder, or minestrone. When developing recipes for this book, my inspirations (besides health) were almost subconscious, even though each soup is very consciously created. In general, my inspirations are guided by seasonal ingredients through my travels, special experiences, and childhood memories, but reinterpreted in a modern way. As you start souping, you will also start recognizing certain veggies and spices in one recipe after another, and then wonder how you never heard of them before. My goal is to introduce you to new ingredients and inspire you to eat in a different way.

The drumroll please . . . here come my soup-er star ingredients. Have fun with them. Go ahead; name-drop them if you have to.

If you don't recognize a particular ingredient, such as kaffir lime, for example, don't fret. Turn to the University of Google or the following descriptions. My recipes are easy to customize, so feel free to play around with the flavors and make your own soup-er creations!

Fungi

Mushrooms have been used in medicine for thousands of years and their benefits have been studied and documented. I first learned how powerful mushrooms were when I was very young; I actually foraged for mushrooms in the woods and still remember ways to recognize edible mushrooms from poisonous. My love affair with fungi has been lifelong and knowing that they heal is just a cherry on top! Chinese Medicine believes in the power of mushrooms, especially when it comes to cancer prevention. You will see that I have shiitake mushrooms in quite a few recipes; I just can't get enough of their goodness. Mushrooms are loaded with nutrients our body needs to generate energy and repair cells, including digestive enzymes, protein, B vitamins, and vitamin D_2. Mushrooms' immune powers are remarkable: They are shown to improve eyesight, headaches, infections, hearing, and the list goes on.

SHIITAKE MUSHROOMS. These antiviral, immune-boosting, cholesterol-lowering fungi are rich in lentinan, a beta-glucan polysaccharide, known for immune boosting properties. Lentinan has been used in Japan as adjuvant therapy for cancer mainly because of its proven tumor regression affect.

WHITE BUTTON MUSHOOMS. Their powers are concentrated in their conjugated linoleic acid (CLA), an important cancer fighter that minimizes the effects of enzyme aromatase, associated with high estrogen levels.

Veggies

ARUGULA AND ROMAINE. These greens alkalize your system, help cleanse and clear your colon as well as provide that bitter taste to help stimulate your liver and gallbladder.

AVOCADO. A precursor for glutathione, it is rich in amino acids needed for effective liver detoxification. Avocado protects against free radical damage, contains powerful anti-inflammatory properties, lowers cholesterol, and is full of phytonutrients that provide numerous other health benefits.

CABBAGE. An excellent anti-inflammatory, cabbage contains lactic acid (which disinfects the colon), phytochemicals (important for cancer prevention), and vitamins A and C that help boost overall health.

CAULIFLOWER. A great source of vitamin K and omega-3 fatty acids, cauliflower is packed with phytonutrients, providing powerful anti-inflammatory and antioxidant support. It lowers our cancer risk by lowering the risk of oxidative stress in our cells.

CELERY. Hippocrates used to prescribe celery to calm the nerves, due to its high calcium level. Rich in trace minerals, which help dilate blood vessels, supporting the transportation of waste from your cells to your liver for removal, every part of celery (including root and seeds) provides your body with alkaline minerals. It purifies the blood, cleanses kidneys, and acts as a liver tonic.

CUCUMBER. Fresh or pickled, cucumber helps flush toxins from your system, reduce heat and inflammation, relieve bad breath, rehydrate your body, and even fight cancers.

DANDELION. Dandelion leaves are used to treat liver problems, kidney diseases, swelling, heartburn, and skin problems. Traditional Chinese Medicine prescribes dandelion for stomach problems and breast inflammation. Dandelion leaves stimulate bile production, helping cleanse and clear the liver and gallbladder.

FENNEL. I love fennel and think that it's so underappreciated. It does wonders for digestion and any tummy issues like gas and bloating. It's extremely cleansing, breaks up kidney stones, purifies the liver, and even expels intestinal worms.

GRAPE LEAVES. A staple of the Mediterranean diet, grape leaves are rich in vitamins A, B_2, B_3, B_6, and B_9, C, E, and K, plus fiber, iron, calcium, magnesium, copper, and manganese. And if that's not enough, they are a surprising source of omega-3 fatty acids, so essentially grape leaves are great for a healthy heart, young-looking body, bright mind, and bone health.

KOHLRABI. This cruciferous vegetable is as cool on the inside as it is on the outside. It contains many of the phytochemicals essential in cancer prevention. It's also a powerful antioxidant because of a high concentration of vitamin C, boosts your immune system, and has lots of fiber.

LEEK. This legendary plant has been around for centuries and its benefits have been lauded for just as long. Leeks have cold- and flu-fighting power, enhance immunity, stimulate appetite, keep blood vessels elastic, and prevent premature aging.

POTATO. These tubers have been vilified in healthy eating circles because of their supposedly high levels of carbohydrates. But in reality, unless you

Soupelina

fry them in massive amounts of oils, potatoes are extremely medicinal. Their nutritional value has been known for centuries; potatoes contain fiber, B vitamins and vitamin C, and minerals. Potatoes are detoxifying, heal stomach ulcers, and are anti-inflammatory. The peels are high in potassium and chlorogenic acid, which can help with cell mutation that causes cancer.

SUNCHOKE. This potato-like flower bud is one of the finest sources of dietary fiber as well as a great source of antioxidant vitamins A, C, and E, iron, and potassium. The dietary fiber acts as a protector against colon cancer and helps eliminate toxic compounds from the gut, while the vitamins and heart-friendly potassium work together to further the cancer-preventative power of this plant as well as reduce blood pressure and risk of viral colds and cough.

SWEET POTATO. Packed with iron and vitamins A, B$_9$, and C, sweet potatoes are known to fight cancer, but also elevate mood and slow down aging. In Chinese medicine, sweet potato has the effect of spleen chi and is believed to prolong life.

WATERCRESS. A rich source of vitamin C, watercress belongs to the mustard family, which gives it antibiotic properties but does not harm our healthy bacteria. It boosts immunity, stimulates digestion, and is believed to remove pimples. Watercress's high potassium content helps you sleep well at night.

WATERMELON RIND. I consider watermelon rind a new superfood and research is here to back it up. Agricultural Research Service of USDA has found that watermelon rinds contain citrulline, an amino acid that removes nitrogen from the blood, stimulates the immune system, and fights cancer.

Sea Veggies

KOMBU AND WAKAME. These staples of Japanese cuisine grow naturally in the deep waters of the ocean. They are used in soups, natural cures, and home remedies because of their rich mineral content and nutritional benefits.

Kombu is known to reduce rates of breast cancer; the lignans in the seaweed are believed to be responsible for the lower rates of the disease in Japanese women who consume kombu on a regular basis. It's good for energy and stomach issues.

Wakame is also rich in iodine, calcium, and vitamins A, B_{12}, C, D, E, and K, and is a powerful immunity booster.

Root Veggies

There is a reason root veggies have been revered in many cultures for centuries. In Chinese Medicine, roots have yang qualities (see page 24) and are some of the more concentrated sources of vitamins and minerals.

BEETS. This superhero veggie is one of the healthiest foods on the planet. My ancestors, Russian centenarians, credit beets (pickled, boiled, and roasted) for their long and healthy lives. Rich in beta-carotene and bioflavonoids, which are essential nutrients for liver detox, beets also protect against heart disease and cancers, especially colon cancer.

CARROTS. Did you know that carrots were first used as medicinal herbs before vegetables? Rich in B vitamins and vitamins A, C, and E, plus phosphorus, potassium, and calcium, carrots are great for liver energy. Carrots cleanse the system and promote healthy skin, hair, and bones. Carrot soup slows down bacterial growth and delivers an abundance of carotenoids, which have been shown to have anticancer effects due to their antioxidant power in reducing free radicals in the body.

CELERIAC ROOT. Just like the top part of the celery plant, the root is rich in trace minerals, which help dilate blood vessels, supporting the transportation of waste from your cells to your liver for removal and providing your body with alkaline minerals.

DAIKON. This large radish is remarkably healing: It aids digestion, cleanses the blood, promotes energy, helps with weight loss, and most important, prevents cancer. As far as cleansing, daikon helps the liver to process toxins, helps kidneys discharge excess water, and dissolves mucus. In Asia, it is believed that daikon helps body burn fat.

GALANGAL. A member of the ginger family, this anti-inflammatory root aids digestion and reduces constipation. In Asia, it is prescribed for congestion and respiratory illnesses. It's also an antioxidant and helps minimize the damage caused by free radicals.

GARLIC. One of the oldest medicinal plants, garlic is an immune system staple, with antifungal, antiviral, and antibacterial properties. In Ayurveda, garlic is prescribed for cancer, and it reduces blood pressure and cholesterol. The garlic must be crushed, chopped, or bruised to access its antibiotic properties.

GINGER helps cleanse and clear your whole digestive tract and is a powerful antibacterial that defends your body from pathogens.

ONION boosts immunity, reduces pain, and has anti-inflammatory properties. Studies show that onions lower cancer risk and increase bone density, especially during menopause. Onion also stimulates production of digestive juices.

Legumes

MUNG BEANS (yellow and green). Known as the "cure-the-sick grain," mung beans hold a special place in East Asian cuisine. They are detoxifying, protein-rich, and chock-full of phosphorus, iron, B vitamins, and vitamins A and C. Mung beans are very important in Ayurveda as they are said to reduce blood fat, suppress tumor growth, protect liver and kidneys, and prevent allergies. For me, it was critical to eat mung beans because of its protease inhibitors that are known to block and prevent formation of tumor cells.

RED AND GREEN LENTILS. High in protein and nutrition, lentils provide your body with the needed amino acids so that it can detox properly. Lentils are also a great source of vitamin B_9, soluble fiber, magnesium, and iron. I can always count on my lentils when my energy levels need a pick-me-up.

TAMARIND. This legume is so good for your digestion and prevention of constipation that you will wonder how you didn't discover it sooner. I love the sour-tart flavor of tamarind and appreciate its antioxidant benefits. In the fall, it's great to protect you from colds.

Citrus

LEMON AND LIME. These fruits kick-start the activity of your liver as well as help stimulate the emptying of your colon. We all know that both lemons and limes are packed with vitamin C, the nutrient that strengthens our immune system. But the benefits don't stop here. Lemons and limes contain twenty-two anticancer compounds, such as limonene, that was shown to slow and even stop the growth of cancer tumors. They also have flavonol glycosides that stop cell division in cancer cells. And even though both are acidic, they actually have an alkalizing effect on our bodily fluids. They clear the body of free radicals and have antiseptic, antiviral, and stimulative properties.

Herbs

Fresh is always best. If that's a tall order, use what you can get, but do consider growing your own herbs. I'm told that it's easy, although I'm not known for my green thumb. You never know how old those store-bought dried herbs are and whether they still have all of their magic. You can also try drying your own herbs and you don't even need any equipment; just place the leaves (without branches) in a cloth bag and keep them in a dry place. With just a few days, you will be the proud maker of your own gourmet dried herbs. I tell you, you will know the difference immediately; your herbs will be bursting with vibrant flavor.

Herbs bring so much depth of flavor to soups, so use them liberally. Try thyme, basil, mint, parsley, cilantro, and fenugreek—you can't go wrong.

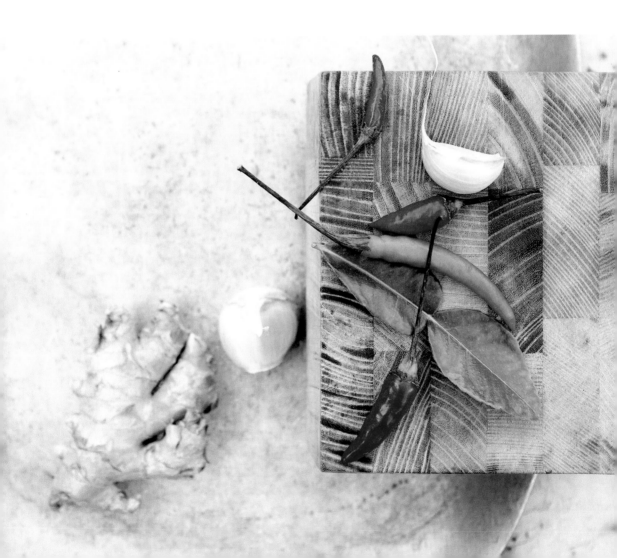

BASIL is a powerful anti-inflammatory herb that will work to help cool and soothe your system, important for cleansing and detoxifying. In Ayurveda, basil is used to treat stomach, kidney, and blood ailments. What I love about basil is that it also affects emotions and can ease sadness.

BAY LEAF elevates your souping by adding depth and aroma. Bay leaf is rich in vitamins A, B$_9$, and C, has immunity-building properties and aids in digestion.

CILANTRO helps pull heavy metals from your system, settle digestion, increase absorption, and relieve intestinal gas or pain.

DILL. Amazing for digestion, insomnia, PMS, and even cancer, this herb has been around for centuries and has always been popular in my family.

FENUGREEK. Another healing herb used as digestive aid, fenugreek stimulates the uterus, reduces blood sugar levels, and lowers cholesterol.

KAFFIR LIME LEAF. This lime is smaller than ones most of us are used to and it has an exotic flavor. Great for digestion, blood, and gum health, the leaf is so popular in Thailand that every home in the countryside is said to

have at least one kaffir lime tree in its yard. If you can't find it in your town's markets, go ahead and use a regular lime. The soup will still taste amazing!

LEMONGRASS has a lot of medicinal qualities: It's used as an astringent, relieves stomach problems and aches, improves circulation and helps with indigestion. Lemongrass is used to treat colds, exhaustion, and even depression. Its essential oil is used in aromatherapy for muscle pain and headaches.

PARSLEY. Rich in vitamins C and K, parsley stimulates circulation and digestion, as well as supports kidneys.

SORREL. Mostly unknown in the United States, sorrel is very popular in Europe and Asia. I love it for its lemony flavor, but once you hear its health benefits, you will be a fan too. It is believed that sorrel strengthens the immune system, builds strong bones, increases energy, and slows the aging process. But it's the cancer-preventative properties that make it so much more valuable! Studies show that sorrel contains polyphenolic compounds, flavonoids, and anthocyanins that seek out free radicals and zap them before they are able to mutate.

THYME is a great antiseptic, antibacterial, and digestive tonic. Besides relieving cough and congestion, thyme contains thymol, an important bioflavonoid with antioxidant properties. Thyme is a good source of calcium, iron, manganese, vitamin K, and fiber.

Spices

BLACK LAVA SALT. Black salt is an Ayurvedic wonder. It's believed to be the most beneficial variety of salt; it doesn't increase the sodium content of your blood, is super cleansing, improves your eyesight, and heals digestive disorders.

CARDAMOM. In Ayurveda, cardamom is prescribed to bring joy and clarity to the mind. It's a stimulating spice that aids your digestive system, detoxifies your body, and opens the flow of energy.

CAYENNE. This heat-giving spice assists digestion by stimulating the flow of saliva and stomach secretions, and it relieves colds, tummy, and bowel problems. The potency is increased when used with garlic, coriander, onion, lemon, and ginger.

CORIANDER. Popular in Indian soups and dhals, coriander stimulates the blood and relieves infections, rashes, gas, and indigestion.

CUMIN. I adore cumin—it's another staple in my kitchen! A digestive aid, cumin is rich in vitamins and minerals, and is an antidote to weakness and fatigue.

HIMALAYAN PINK SALT. Containing all 84 essential trace minerals the body needs to thrive, this salt will help alkalize your body, increase hydration, prevent muscle cramping, strengthen bones, lower blood pressure, and dissolve and eliminate sediment to remove toxins.

MUSTARD SEEDS. This spice has strong anticancer properties due to the presence of glucosinolates known to inhibit the growth of cancer cells. I also love mustard seeds for their antioxidant properties, beauty benefits (skin hydration from within), and infection-fighting benefits.

SAFFRON. Saffron golden threads are expensive to harvest, making this spice a very special one in your kitchen. But a little goes a long way when it comes to saffron, a prized plant in Ayurvedic medicine for its medicinal and aphrodisiac properties. From aiding digestion and improving appetite to anemia, depression, insomnia, and even infertility, saffron is the bomb!

TURMERIC. The number-one spice in my kitchen! The moment I discovered this golden spice, it was love at first sight! For centuries turmeric has been used to heal the digestive system; it's good for your heart, brain function, and joint health. It's anti-inflammatory and antioxidant, it destroys cancer cells, and it's antiaging!

Oils

COCONUT OIL. Hailed as a superfood, coconut oil has so many health benefits that I use it for everything, from boosting my metabolism to cooking to massaging my body. Lauric acid in coconut oil is what makes it so special (it's a fat that can be found in breast milk and we all know how good breast milk is for babies). Our body converts lauric acid into monolaurin, which has antimicrobial, anti-fungal, antibacterial, and soothing properties.

EXTRA-VIRGIN OLIVE OIL. So much scientific research has been done on EVOO, but it was the ancient Greeks who started the trend: They took 1 to 2 spoonfuls of oil every morning to help with healthy bowels and digestion. Our body easily digests olive oil, rich in vitamin E and phenols, but its chlorophyll is what facilitates the cleansing of the gall bladder. Make sure you buy certified organic cold-pressed EVOO.

SESAME OIL. If you haven't discovered sesame oil yet, you are about to fall in love. Besides its intense flavors, it's one of the most nutrient-dense foods out there (along with sesame seeds). Rich in iron, calcium, magnesium, zinc, and tryptophan, sesame oil prevents cancer, boosts bone health, lowers blood pressure, promotes heart and oral health, protects against DNA damage, and boosts digestive health.

Are You NUTS?

I love a good nut. It's a satisfying snack, full of important vitamins, minerals, and good fats. But in cleansing, nuts are a no-no in my book. Nuts are not easy to digest; they are actually resistant to digestion due to the tough walls of their cells. As much as one-fifth of the fat in nuts never gets absorbed by the body, according to a nutrition scientist from Purdue University, Dr. Richard Mattes. Allergies to nuts are also some of the most common causes of intestinal problems. And according to the Cleveland Clinic, nuts may cause intestinal issues due to their salicylates, which can irritate the digestive tract of some people. With all the seasonal goodness available to us, why go nuts?

Fruits are the bomb! I get so excited when berries, peaches, and cherries are in season. What can be better than a ripe juicy peach or a slice of refreshing watermelon during the day? But fruits are also full of sugar (good for you, but still), can give you blood sugar spikes, and digestion-wise break down differently in your stomach, thus competing with veggies if eaten together. So, if you are not a fan of bloating or gas, eat a piece of fruit alone before your veggie soup. Oh, and tomato is actually a "veggie fruit" and okay to play with other veggies in a soup.

Soy is so controversial; after reading dozens out of thousands of contradictory studies that have been published on soy, I decided that it's safer and more healing not to have soy in my soups. Now, fermented soy is a different story, because it has a probiotic effect that is easy for your body to digest and absorb. For centuries Asian cultures have been eating such fermented soy products as miso and tempeh, reaping the health benefits from them. The rest of soy is iffy, and so I stay away from it.

4

SOUP-RISES

If you've never done a soup cleanse before, relax; it's not that hard. You won't feel starved, cold, and depleted. In fact, everyone who tries a Soupelina cleanse raves about feeling warm, loved, and uplifted. The soup cleanse is designed to help you heal and kick-start a healthy lifestyle. It's not about creating additional stress, it's about de-stressing you and creating peace within you.

And like I said earlier: You don't have to count calories! I hate counting calories! Who cares about calories? We've been brainwashed to worry about every morsel that goes into our body, but they forgot to tell us that what we need to be counting is nutrients! That's your number-one task now: Every single thing you put in your mouth from now on has to be filled with nutrients. And flavor! And you can have as much of this good stuff as you like.

Now that this pressure is off your table, let's talk souping. For many, the cleanse will be a smooth ride, although some will have road humps and even bumps, emotional detours, and cravings a-plenty, especially in the first couple of days and nights. Because it's just not easy to give up eating crap—and at first your body is still not sure you are trying to get healthy. You need to train it.

What I'm most excited about for you are the surprising benefits you will get from the cleanse. Until then, there are still a few things you just gotta do.

+ Make a plan.

Planning is important to avoid bumps and detours. Although souping is a relatively easy transition, it really depends on what you've been eating before. First, decide on how many days you want to cleanse. Start with a 3-Day Boost Cleanse (page 90) and see how you do.

You will not eat out; there are no quick-fixes or short stops at the favorite café. All the soups require advance prep and planning: fermentation, broth making, soaking legumes. If you are not an avid planner, this is another transition.

+ Prepare your kitchen.

Do you have all the tools and ingredients for the days you plan to cleanse? Try not to leave it to the last minute or think that you can get home early and cook the soup. Prepare all the meals for the day ahead. Carry a cooler with you if you think you might get stuck in traffic or get called into a meeting. There is nothing worse than feeling guilty when you start out on a high note and then stumble because, let's face it, life happens.

+ Prepare your body.

You're probably wondering, *Can I go into a cleanse cold tofurkey or do I need a few days to warm up?* It all depends on where you are right now. If you are a healthy eater, then jump right in. But if you indulge in a glass of wine every night, enjoy cheese and bread . . . not to mention chocolate and French fries, then you might need a week to wean yourself off. First, reduce your meat consumption to only twice that week, and completely cut out dairy, alcohol, processed sugar, and refined carbs. Cut back on coffee to one cup a day for the first three days and then drink green tea instead for the rest of the week. Increase your veggie intake and go ahead, have a few soups.

To treat yourself during the cleanse, book your massage appointments. Also, make sure to book your colonics (I will discuss that in Chapter 5) and buy an enema bag.

+ Prepare your mind.

As you get souping, you might have voices in your head whispering, "Oh, one slice of this freshly baked sourdough bread won't hurt" or "I'll just try it another day . . . it doesn't really matter." But it does matter and you have the power to quiet that voice and tell yourself that what you are doing is the best for your body and your health, and your success is worth the commitment you made. If you get cravings, remind yourself that this is your new way of enjoying real foods, and not a deprivation. If you haven't already, start journaling. This is a great way to set goals and intentions and pour out any questions or **frustrations or** successes.

+ Expect detox reactions.

You are excited about eating better, but you are not feeling your best. Nothing is wrong; your body is just adjusting. When you cleanse, you flush out excess toxins and as a result you experience a temporary cleansing reaction. It even has a name, the Herxheimer effect, named after Dr. Karl Herxheimer who discovered it in the early 1900s and said that the short-term symptoms are actually a sign of healing.

Expect and welcome the detox symptoms; they're a sign your body is moving forward. It is common to feel as if you are getting a flu, with runny nose, headaches, joint and muscle pain, aches, sweating, sore throat, chills, nausea, irritability, and even rashes. The reaction usually lasts for two to three days.

+ Be patient.

Breathe if you feel tired or cranky. It will pass. If your gym has a sauna or a steam room, go get some steam; it's a good way to encourage deep sweating to release toxins through the skin. Call a friend to chat about what you are going through or just take an extra nap. Everyone is different. I jump in all the way, while others need some time. Some people feel better right away; for others, it takes a week or two. Remember, it takes time, so don't expect miracles immediately. Allow yourself to be surprised.

+ Tell the world.

You've seen celebrities tweet and Instagram photos of themselves with healthy foods, detailing every step of their healthy detoxes. Use them as your inspiration! This will help you stay on track because you will feel responsible. It's a great trick I discovered a long time ago. The moment you tell someone you are not having dessert today, you feel much stronger to stick to your guns. Besides, it's great for your image. Watch your friends text you because they will want what you are having.

GAPS, FODMaP, and Other Specialized Diets

Although all of the recipes in the book are 100 percent vegan and call for organic, GMO- and gluten-free ingredients, and not a single one includes sugar, fruits, soy, or nuts, you might be like one of my Soupelina customers healing with the GAPS or FODMaP diet or any other specialized program that suggests avoiding certain veggies and legumes, such as onions and garlic. You can still make the soup you like and reap all the benefits plus enjoy the taste, without onions and garlic. If an essential ingredient is not something you can eat, substitute or move on to a different soup recipe.

The Best Soup-rises

Becoming a soup gourmand after your first cleanse is one of the big surprises you will get. But there is more.

+ You will feel better than you've felt in a long time.

After your short detox reaction (which you might not even experience), you will feel as if you can fly. I will never forget my first cleanse, when the morning after quite severe detox reactions, I woke up and saw brightness. I never felt that kind of clarity before. It was exhilarating and exciting! Get ready for it!

+ You won't feel hungry.

I was expecting to have cravings for my favorite foods and one of my biggest fears was that I would be hungry all the time. In fact, the day before my first cleanse, I did something I've never done before: I bought all kinds of sugary treats I never even liked because I was so worried I would be miserable. It's scary to put our vices on the back burner for a while. I was surprised that I felt I was eating too much and I was never hungry. Besides, it was kind of fun to tell my friends I was on a new soup cleansing thing and what a great challenge it was.

+ What was once foreign will become familiar.

Oh, the places you'll go after you complete your first soup cleanse! I learned about many of the ingredients in my soups from my international travels, but I have to admit, I still had to Google some of them. You will feel as if you are living in a foreign land for a bit, but in just a matter of weeks you will learn how to spell *Ayurveda*, ferment Rejuvelak, and even make kvass.

+ You will never have to worry about what's for breakfast again.
Because the answer will be—SOUP! Your family and friends might think you are crazy, but watch them join in and enjoy the ride.

+ You will improve your mood.
You might be cranky at the beginning, but as you settle into your new life-style, you will feel so good about yourself that nothing will be able to stop you or even slow you down. Watch you being kinder to yourself, nicer to others, and tolerant of those you had no time for before.

+ Your anxiety will go away.
Experiencing new people, foods, and places without tormenting nervousness is the new normal. Get used to it. Say good-bye to your insecurities, wave farewell to paranoia; you will feel cool as a cucumber, and calm, too. You will rediscover your "gut feeling"!

+ You will most likely notice emotional release.
Feelings you've held onto for years will spill out along with the toxins the moment you cut out all processed, unhealthy foods. You might suddenly burst into tears or feel upset for no apparent reason. Allow it to happen and accept it if and when it does. Go ahead and cry. Yell if you have to! You will feel so much better when it passes.

+ You will enjoy cooking.
Eating out will still be fun, but now you will know better. You will research the restaurants before going, check where it gets its produce, and won't settle for conventional anymore. Cooking will become an adventure. You will fall in love with discovering new ingredients and spending your weekends in the farmers markets and kitchen instead of a mall.

+ You will start creating your own recipes and host soup parties.
I want an invitation! Because I know you will become the star in your family

and circle of friends. Your kids will love you and the soups you create; their friends will be hanging out at your house because their moms get take-out. And before you know it, soup parties will be famous in your town.

+ Your tastes will change.
I bet you didn't expect that! You won't crave fatty-salty-sugary foods anymore, and when you are at that fancy office party, I swear you will turn away the tray with baked cheesy puffs. Because you know that even one bite will taste weird.

FAQs

+ How long in advance can I make my soups?
You can make all soups on a Sunday for the entire 5-Day Cleanse. Raw soups should be made each day and eaten that day.

+ What do I carry them in?
You can buy soup containers at www.soupelina.com, carry your soups in coffee cups, or place them in glass jars. Glass jars are my least favorite for transporting because of possible breakage and the heat factor (they get hot when reheating or carrying a hot soup). Another idea is buying a thermos that will keep your soups hot throughout the day.

+ Can I freeze my soups?
Of course, you can! But why? There is nothing tastier than a pot of fresh soup on the stove and a bowl immediately after it's been cooked. It's more nutrient-rich, too. But if you do decide to freeze, divide the soup into portions to give yourself flexibility. Soups are easily defrosted if you just let them sit on the counter for a couple of hours or pop the frozen block into a pot and warm slowly.

+ Do I peel my veggies when cooking?
If you buy organic produce, you don't have to peel. Make sure you wash them thoroughly and scrub root veggies with a brush. Nonorganic veggies should be peeled and washed properly.

+ Can I eat something else if I get hungry?

You can have as much broth as you like. For the "chew" factor, load your broth with fresh herbs, veggies, and sprouts. Keep drinking water, lemon water, herbal tea, and Rejuvelak throughout the day (see page 190 for an easy Rejuvelak recipe). Munch on sprouts, Persian cucumbers, and seaweed.

+ Can I just pick one or two soups instead of cooking four or five?

It's best to mix up the recipes so you don't get bored; also, your body needs different vitamins and minerals for optimum health. Give yourself a balanced nutrition and enjoy the process.

+ Will I get enough protein?

Can we all stop worrying about protein? Most Americans get way more protein than we need, five times more, in fact! It's fiber we need to be concerned about. Fiber is what keeps our digestion working and we are all deficient. Soups are a great source of protein: Between green leafy veggies, legumes, and mushrooms, you are more than meeting your protein needs.

+ How much exercise should I do during the cleanse?

The soup cleanse is the time for your body to relax and nourish itself. Be gentle to yourself: Don't engage in rigorous workouts, but light yoga is great. Avoid hot yoga, though.

+ Should I take supplements during the soup cleanse?

You will be getting plenty of vitamins and nutrients through your soups, but I do like my vitamin D_3, unless I'm on the beach all week. If you are not drinking Rejuvelak, take at least one probiotic in the morning.

+ How much weight will I lose on a 5-Day Cleanse?

It varies per person, but on average it's about a pound per day. Much of it is retained water and built-up food matter in the colon. To maintain weight loss, incorporate souping into your new healthy lifestyle.

A WORD ABOUT FIBER AND PROTEIN

If you're a plant-powered babe like myself, you know that every time others hear you don't eat meat or cheese, they ask you where you get your protein. Come on, people! Multiple studies have shown that an average American takes in 120 to 150 grams of protein each day, while the USDA recommends about 46 grams. But experts who study nutrition and its links to diseases, such as Dr. Joel Fuhrman (oh, I wish we were related!) suggest consuming only 20 to 35 grams of protein per day. What this means is that we have been overdosing on protein and the consequences are right in front of us: We get sicker and sicker. A low-protein diet is now widely accepted to be the healthiest.

But let's talk fiber, a.k.a. plant roughage (the cell walls of veggies, the bran of grains, and the pulp of fruits that don't get digested). I admit fiber doesn't sound sexy, but it is your friend because it helps you look and feel sexier. Fiber cleans out your digestive system, helps maintain healthy bowels, and pushes out all those toxins, waste, and cholesterol. That creates beautiful flora for your gut, bolsters your immunity, helps regulate blood sugar, and protects your heart. Research has shown that dietary fiber may also provide protection against several kinds of cancer, such as breast, colon, stomach, ovary, rectum, mouth, endometrium, and pharynx. The research has prompted the American Cancer Society to advocate for 30 percent more of the recommended daily fiber intake, which is now 25 to 38 grams per day. Sadly, our average fiber intake is roughly half that.

5

SOUPELINA SECRETS— MAKE IT YOUR SOUP CLEANSE

I have to let you in on my secret. Pinky promise you won't tell?

I don't like rules. I like to break them. And I'm really good at making up my own rules. Say what? What does that have to do with souping, you ask?

I tell you this because I don't want you to carefully follow my advice. Don't read this book and start doing exactly what I say. Use it as a tool in your own journey to health. I just want you to know the facts. I'm a big believer that knowledge trumps rules. You know what they say: Knowledge is power.

I want you to have fun in the kitchen. My recipes are just recommendations. Be adventurous, experiment with new ingredients, make these recipes work for *you*. Don't worry if you feel like altering them. **It's *your* soup cleanse, so *you* get to call the shots.**

The good thing about soup is that it doesn't demand exact measurements. That's why I describe veggies as small, medium, and large, not by how much they weigh. Salt and spiciness are personal, so taste, correct if need be, and enjoy. When I cook at home, I rarely measure, and once you get the hang of this souping thing, you will be a pro, too. It's not brain surgery, but I can't say that it doesn't help our brain.

Please don't worry if one batch is different from another; it's normal. It used to freak me out, too. Organic veggies are real, just like us humans. When the sun gives them more love, they taste sweeter; when it rains more, they are plumper. Accept and appreciate their imperfections; that's the beauty of real food!

Souping is unlike any other cooking. It's slow. It's imperfect. It's satisfying. For me, it's also meditative; souping helped me to reconnect with myself. I love watching soup cook and mature from a bunch of veggies and spices into a beautiful creation. I also incorporated a few tricks into my soup cleanse to get the most out of my experience. And I can't wait to share them with you.

Join our Instagram, Facebook, and Twitter community for inspiration, love, recipes, and tips.

www.instagram.com/soupelinala
www.facebook.com/soupelina
www.twitter.com/soupelinala

HOW I FOOL MY CRAVINGS

Don't go off the detox rails when cravings come knocking. Here are my tricks to beating the midnight binge.

+ Sip a hot fresh mint and lemongrass tea.

+ Enjoy a handful of sunflower seeds.

+ Grab an organic Granny Smith apple.

+ Go for a handful of berries.

+ Drink lemon water.

+ Make a fancy plate with fresh cucumbers and radishes.

+ Indulge in kale chips.

+ Get more sleep.

Cooking Secrets

+ Start with pure water for the best base.

+ Use only organic ingredients.

+ Sweat or sauté the aromatics to deepen the flavor.

+ Use the right tools.

+ Add the salt gradually as you cook.

+ Punch up the flavor with fresh herbs.

+ Garnish like a pro.

Clean Up Your Act

Colon cleansing and enemas may sound scary, but they are critical to your new healthy bod. They've been around since the Egyptians and have been widely administered by doctors for centuries. And they take your soup cleansing up a notch. It's so much more natural than taking laxatives that can irritate and even dehydrate your colon.

+ Enemas (and implants)

Enemas and implants get the lower part of your colon toned and strong. All you have to do is lie on a nice towel in the bathroom with a pillow under your tush (I like to light a candle and dim the lights, too), relax, slide the tube up, and let the liquid flow.

To get the enema bag ready, fill it with 1 or 2 quarts of lukewarm filtered or distilled water, lubricate the tube (coconut oil is best; do not use Vaseline or other petroleum products), hang the bag on a doorknob or a towel rack, and open the clamp. Lie on your left side with your knees bent. The tube doesn't need to go in far; 3 to 4 inches will do. To get the most benefit, let the water flow slowly until you feel full, then clamp off and relax. Let the water circulate in your colon, give it some help with a self-massage of your tummy. You can also roll onto your right side to allow the water to hit other areas. Try to hold the water for 10 to 15 minutes before releasing it into a toilet bowl. Never force it to stay in.

When you are finished with your enema, get ready for an implant. "What the heck is that?" you ask. I describe implants as enema sidekicks; they are a great way to nourish the body after an enema. Since I'm a huge believer in the power of wheatgrass, I recommend wheatgrass implants to strengthen the colon as well as the liver. Sending wheatgrass up your colon is a great way to add oxygen to your blood and energy to your body. A single 4-ounce shot juiced at home or bought at a juice bar is like a power shot. Just place it into your enema bag, let it flow into your lower bowel and then hold it for about 20 minutes. It doesn't always work like that because all that chlorophyll and oxygen makes you want to go like crazy. Hold it as long as you can. You can lie on your back, prop your legs, read a book, breathe . . . just hold it. It pulls so much stuff off your colon walls and helps restore an electrolyte balance. Wheatgrass implants also accelerate cleansing and healing of the lower bowel.

+ Colon Hydrotherapy

Colon hydrotherapy is one continuous enema administered by a therapist, during which water is introduced to the entire length of the colon. It's one of my favorite things, no joke. You feel clean and squeaky when you are done.

+ Oil Pulling

Oil pulling is the ancient detox method that you may have heard a lot about lately. An Ayurvedic technique, swishing a tablespoon of coconut or sesame oil for about 20 minutes and then spitting it out, absorbs microbial bacteria in the mouth. The practice originated in India thousands of years ago and promotes optimal health. It's been increasingly popular, as the detox movement has gained momentum, and now recent studies show that oil pulling helps protect against gingivitis and microorganisms that cause bad breath. It is also believed that oil pulling prevents many conditions from sinusitis to digestion, from mood swings to chronic disease. It makes sense, since a healthy mouth is a gateway to healthy digestion, a healthy brain, and a healthy body. Just don't swallow the oil during or after swishing; simply spit it into the trash (not into the sink because oil could clog your pipes!) and brush your teeth. I swish my mouth with water and apple cider vinegar for extra benefits before I brush. To get the most out of oil pulling, you should pull first thing in the morning before drinking or brushing.

I always felt that we don't pay enough attention to our oral health and see beautiful teeth and gums as more of a cosmetic enhancement than a sign of health. Oil pulling is one of the easiest things you can do for your health. And I promise you will love what it will do for you.

Beyond Skin Deep

Lavender to relax frazzled nerves, lemongrass to soothe stressed senses and regular massages to feel happier—self-pampering during your cleanse is what's it all about. In all pursuits of well-being, these simple techniques practiced often are more rewarding and effective than vacations. Go ahead, walk the path that brings a bounty of healing.

+ Dry Skin Brushing

Dry skin brushing supports optimal detoxification, as it sloughs off dead skin cells and activates waste removal through your lymph nodes. You are releasing toxins during the cleanse, so you gotta make sure they have an easy way of coming out. You know that skin is our largest organ and if it can't eliminate the dumped waste efficiently, why go through all the trouble?

Simply get a natural bristle brush—they are very easy to find, from on-line to your local drugstore; I also like using loofah gloves: You get the job done faster if you put these on both hands. Most dry brushing devotees recommend that you brush in upward strokes, focusing in particular on areas where the major lymph nodes are located (armpits, groin, base of the neck). Go crazy; it feels amazing! To dry brush properly, brush your entire body, including the soles of your feet, except for your face and private parts. Your skin should be pink after a brush, but not red or irritated.

Dry brushing will move your lymphatic fluid, stimulate your immune system, wake up your circulation, and make your skin feel soft. The best time to dry brush is first thing in the morning before you shower, while you are oil pulling. Try it once and you will be hooked. You will also feel energized and excited about your day.

+ Aromatherapy

Aromatherapy can help you to stay positive and calm during the cleanse. Another ancient practice, dating back to the Egyptian times, it promotes mental, spiritual, and physical health, and it uses plants' essential oils. A

French chemist, René-Maurice Gattefossé, who coined the term *aromatherapy*, discovered that different oils had different healing properties, such as antiseptic, antitoxic, calming, and stimulating. They activate nerve cells in our olfactory system that sends impulses to the brain, stimulating our immune, circulatory, and nervous systems. Pretty impressive, right?!

I'm constantly amazed how healing plants are. We can eat them, drink them, smell them, use them to massage our skin . . . all while they heal us. New research shows that essential oils even kill "superbugs," such as staph infections, *E. coli*, and many other bacteria and fungi.

Essential oils are like an extra set of helpers during your cleanse. I love alternating lemongrass and eucalyptus oil in my diffuser during the day; it helps me stay focused, calm, and ache-free. At night, I fall asleep to lavender oil and sometimes I massage my upper chest area with a few drops. I have a few other favorite essential oils that are wonderful in ridding the body of toxic waste and negative thoughts, and making your cleanse not only taste but smell yummy, too. The following are some of my favorite oils; you can find them online and in natural food stores.

Peppermint oil: You can add a few drops to your coconut oil during the oil pull. Not only will it make your mouth feel fresh, it will soothe your digestive system and help you with staying focused.

Rosemary oil: Take a bath with it and then add a few drops to coconut oil and massage it into your body. Your digestion will improve, your circulation will crank up, and—get this—your memory will improve, too! It's also great if you are experiencing detox symptoms, such as draining sinuses.

Lemon oil has its astringent properties; there is even a cleanse that calls for lemon oil in cooking. I use it because lemon oil is said to prevent cancer, free up the lymphatic and respiratory systems, and reduce inflammation.

+ Infrared Sauna
Infrared sauna is another great way to help your detox efforts. You can never do too much to cleanse your body. Infrared saunas are not your regular dry heat saunas, which are excellent for your liver and gallbladder. Infrared saunas'

heat goes deeper, helping your body release toxins, including heavy metals and toxins from chemotherapy and radiation treatments. It also promotes relaxation by balancing cortisol levels and burns up to 700 calories in one session by getting your heart to beat faster. Check your local acupuncturist offices and wellness clinics; they usually have infrared saunas on their premises. If you can spring for it, invest in one. It's a great thing to have at home.

+ Massage

Massage is not just for pampering. I'm not really sure why it's not covered by our health insurance; its tangible health benefits have been known for centuries. But we are just beginning to study massage and already research shows that massage boosts immune function in women with breast cancer, improves symptoms in kids with asthma, helps with pain, and eliminates toxins. What's not to love? I'm a big proponent of lymphatic drainage massage, especially during a cleanse. I used to feel guilty and frivolous when I would pay for massage. *There are so many important things I need to pay for*, I would tell myself. But not anymore. Massage is an integral part of healing, not a luxury splurge.

The Fountain of Youth

There is nothing like a good night's sleep to reinvigorate you to face life head-on. Combined with a few other indulgencies, you actually allow your body to take care of you. It's especially effective during a cleanse; the moment you consciously give your body permission to take care of you, you will be amazed at what it can do.

+ Bathing

Bathing is great to unwind after each day of cleansing. If you decided to give aromatherapy a try and have a few of your favorite essential oils, bath time will become a relaxing ritual. Add a few drops of lavender or eucalyptus oil and watch your stress melt away. Add 1 or 2 cups of Epsom salts and you will have a remedy for detoxing. Relaxing in a warm bathtub is also a natural way to induce sleep, an important part of any cleanse. Don't forget to dim the light, light a few candles, and turn on your slow tunes.

+ Sleep

Sleep is the time when your body can repair damage caused by stress and harmful exposures. Our cells produce more protein while we sleep and those protein molecules form the building blocks for cells. Who doesn't talk about getting enough sleep these days? But are you actually getting enough sleep? You decided to make healthy changes and cleanse your body, please make sure you take care of your temple and let it rest: It's been doing so much for you. Skip TV and any technology during your cleanse; use the freed time to sleep and think. You won't believe how recharged you will feel in just a couple of days. But sleeping at night is not enough; take naps during the day. I used to be very antinap; who has the time? But nowadays I'm in love with siesta; anytime I can snooze for fifteen minutes, I do it!

+ "Me" Time

"Me" time is no longer optional in my book. When I was diagnosed, I was told by doctors that I had to start paying attention to me. Wait, what? How about all my obligations, duties, and responsibilities? The truth is, we all have fifteen to thirty minutes every day to kick back and relax. Don't skip on it! Whether it's taking a bath or reading a book, calling a friend or meditating, taking "me" time is an important time for transformation.

+ Hyperbaric Oxygen Therapy (HBOT)

HBOT is something you might have to research and not every city will have it. But if you do, you are in major luck! I'm obsessed with hyperbaric therapy! It was Dr. Agolli who first had me spend an hour a day for four straight days in a hyperbaric chamber. I swear I felt that I was on the set of a sci-fi movie. But Dr. Agolli explained to me how much power this oxygen-rich, high-pressure cylindrical chamber had in my healing. When the chamber is closed, you feel as if you are taking off on a plane, because you are breathing 100 percent pure oxygen delivered under high pressure. It boosts your natural healing process by promoting the growth of new blood vessels, especially in areas that need healing and allows your body to absorb the molecules easily, stimulating the growth of new healthy tissue. It was great for me after radiation treatments, because radiation is known for damaging the tiny blood vessels that feed the cells. Plus, as part of cleansing, it helped repair the damage.

6

TIME TO SOUP

Are you excited? Your healing journey is about to begin. Whether you are cleansing for three days, a week, or a whole month, or are dipping your toes in with a one-day reset, at the end of it, you will emerge with more energy, fewer headaches, less fatigue and crankiness, glowing skin, and uplifted spirit.

You can lean on me virtually or join the community cleanse boards for mental support, but most important, record your efforts, bumps, and triumphs in a special journal.

Take a before photo of yourself—a selfie will do—and write down your first journal entry: What is the purpose for your cleanse? Revisit this page often; it will help you refocus if you hit a bump or feel like cheating.

Okay, let's get souping!

The Cleanses

Besides the seasonal 5-Day Soup Cleanses, I designed a 24-Hour Reset Cleanse and a 3-Day Boost Cleanse for those times when you need a quick pick-me-up but can't commit for longer. The Reset Cleanse is completely raw and will infuse your body with plant goodness, reduce bloating and give you instant energy. The Boost Cleanse is an easy three-day gourmet feast that will nourish you, give your tummy a break from daily indulgencies, and kick-start healthy habits.

A DAY IN THE LIFE OF SOUPING

Open your eyes and spend the first five minutes of your day visualizing what makes you happy. Run a mental list of things you are grateful for. Get a spoonful of coconut oil and start your daily oil pulling. While you are swishing the oil in your mouth, dry brush your skin and take a shower. Brush your teeth, drink a large glass of filtered or spring water with lemon, and head to the kitchen for your first soup. Eat every three hours throughout the day to keep your metabolism working. Do not skip meals. And do not eat within three hours of going to sleep. Drink plenty of water between meals and especially during any workouts (remember—keep it light!). For better digestion do not drink water with your meals. Breakfast, lunch, and dinner are your veggie soups; broths are your snacks. Take a warm bath with essential oils before bedtime, write in your health journal, and then spend five minutes visualizing something that makes you happy, the same thing you did when you woke up. That's a full day!

Remember to rest and nourish yourself during the cleanse, even if it's just for a day. Take extra time to sleep, read, meditate, and take a bath; the more rest you get, the more beneficial the detox.

If you are a soup cleanse virgin, I suggest you take a few days to prepare yourself. Your body needs to be ready for the flood of all the detoxifying nutrients, minerals, and enzymes. Take a good look at your fridge and your pantry. Do you have coffee there? How about alcohol? Sugar, animal products, processed and fried foods, wheat, and cigarettes have to go, too. Spend these couple of prep days eating lightly cooked foods, salads, and whole grains, and drink tea and lots of water. This gently eases your body into your cleanse.

The key to success with Soupelina Soup Cleanse is making it work for your unique needs and goals. Whether you just want a one-day tune-up, a three- or five-day detox, or a longer regenerating soup lifestyle, the suggested menus and recipes will help you to create your own soup plan for life. The idea is to create an optimum environment for your body to heal itself. You won't know how much more healthy you can feel until you embark on a soup lifestyle. Make this cleanse your own by changing up recipes, swapping soups in the suggested menus, and just having a good time.

And one more thing: If you are ill or recovering from a serious health condition, consider incorporating soups into your daily life. I will have more on that in the next chapter, with tips on how to continue your healing diet.

The 5-Day Soup Cleanse: Sample Menus

I promise you will fall in love with the clarity cleansing will bring to your life and enjoy shaking up your routine. I designed the 5-Day Soup Cleanse to rebuild and regenerate your body while eliminating environmental and metabolic toxins. This is a great cleanse to keep your heart healthy, reduce your cholesterol levels, and achieve normal blood pressure levels. The fiber-rich cleanse works on a cellular level and by the end of the cleanse, your spiritual energy will increase and you will feel lighter, happier, and more alive.

What Will It Do for Me?

You will most likely lose a few pounds and have a flatter tummy. Your poo will be regular and you will eliminate several times per day. You will get rid of the minor health issues, such as fatigue, headaches, abdominal discomfort, and muscle aches. But my favorite benefit from this cleanse is a state of calm and being at peace with yourself. You will release old emotions and bring in new healthy feelings.

You've heard of spring cleaning. Now you will start spring cleansing. According to Chinese Medicine, spring is the best season for a deep liver detox to enhance its function. The expansive spring energy helps move things to the surface to prepare for the high activity of summer.

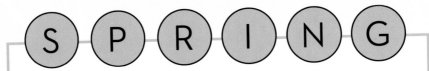

SPRING

BREAKFAST

You're My Fava-rite!

MIDMORNING SNACK

Lemongrass Cleansing Broth

LUNCH

Mint, Take a Hint!

MIDAFTERNOON SNACK

Shake Your Tamarind

DINNER

That's Just Dandy!

SUMMER

Summer brings extra heat to the body and often gets us out of balance. It's best to cleanse with simple soups full of nutrients and fiber to provide the body with ideal energy.

BREAKFAST

Easy Peas-y

MIDMORNING SNACK

Macho Gazpacho

LUNCH

And the Beet Goes On

MIDAFTERNOON SNACK

Veggie Healing Broth

DINNER

Cauliflower Me, Maybe?!

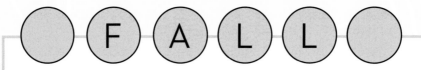

FALL

The fall cleanse focuses on cleansing the large intestine and the lungs. This is the time to cleanse with richer and heartier soups, take in vital energy from the harvest, and release what's not needed.

BREAKFAST
. . . .

Guys and Dhals

MIDMORNING SNACK
. . . .

Coconut Galangal Broth

LUNCH
. . . .

I'll Be Bok, Choy!

MIDAFTERNOON SNACK
. . . .

Lemongrass Cleansing Broth

DINNER
. . . .

Lentil Me Entertain You

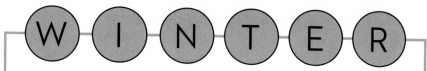

WINTER

The winter cleanse focuses on keeping the energy levels and strong immune system to protect us from getting sick. We need warm, robust foods during the winter months because we feel hungrier in colder weather and need higher body temperature, which means consuming more energy.

BREAKFAST
• • • • • • • • • • •

Oh Dhal-ing!

MIDMORNING SNACK
• •

Magic Turmeric Broth

LUNCH
• • • • • • • •

I Don't Carrot All What They Say

MIDAFTERNOON SNACK
• •

Pho Sho

DINNER
• • • • • • • •

I Gotcha Kabocha Covered

FOR EXPERT CLEANSERS

+ Drink 2 ounces of freshly squeezed wheatgrass juice twice a day. Do not chase wheatgrass with orange or any fruit. If you have a hard time with wheatgrass juice, chew a slice of raw ginger before the shot or sprinkle some ground cinnamon on your tongue immediately afterward. Allow one hour after your wheatgrass shot to digest it, before eating anything.

+ Drink 32 ounces of Rejuvelak (page 190) throughout the day to help digestion. Rejuvelak is fermented quinoa drink and it populates your tummy with good bacteria and enzymes, plus prevents overgrowth of bad bacteria and candida.

+ Do one enema and two wheatgrass implants daily until your colon is clean. You will know your colon is clean when you eliminate the food you recently digested.

24-Hour Raw Reset Cleanse

This cleanse is designed as a tune-up and will recharge you within just one day. All the ingredients for the soups are whole, living foods, full of living energy and nutrients. This is a beautiful opportunity for you to break free from crappy or restaurant foods and provide your body with real foods for a day. To get maximum benefit, the soups have to be prepared fresh and eaten immediately after preparation, so I suggest you do this cleanse over a weekend or when you have a day to pamper yourself. Remember, this will not be hard! You are welcome to continue this cleanse for an extra day for a weekend.

You know that I prefer cooked soups over raw soups, but I do make exceptions for short cleanses. The raw cleanse is best for spring and summer seasonal cleanses, stick with hot soups for your fall and winter cleanses.

WHAT WILL IT DO FOR ME?

Your digestive system will thank you for a day of high fiber, which will strengthen your bowel's peristaltic action and result in a satisfying poo. The fiber will also get rid of the waste attached to your intestinal lining. And your liver gets a day off from processing all the foods you've been eating before. There you go!

UPON WAKING

2 ounces Wheatgrass Shot

BREAKFAST

What the Hemp?

MIDMORNING SNACK

Thai Me Up, Thai Me Down Gazpacho

LUNCH

A-Lotta Avocado

MIDAFTERNOON SNACK

Macho Gazpacho

DINNER

I'm Pumpkin Myself Up

Soupelina
soup Cleanse
MENU

Enjoy your soup cleanse!

XO Soupelina

Left to right: Thai Me Up, Thai
Me Down Gazpacho, page 197;
I'm Pumpkin Myself Up, page 195;
A-Lotta Avocado, page 200; Macho
Gazpacho, page 201; What the
Hemp? page 195

3-Day Boost Cleanse

This year-round plan will give your body an opportunity to strengthen your digestion and cellular metabolism, to create and maintain healthy tissue, plus help restore your body's balance. The cleanse will also enhance your liver's ability to detoxify and your intestinal tract's natural ability to eliminate toxins.

WHAT WILL IT DO FOR ME?

All the soups are low on the glycemic index, so you will lose a little weight and feel more toned. You will also feel more balanced and energetic. Your eyes will sparkle, you will feel more energy, and you will feel more alive.

BREAKFAST

· · · · · · · · · · ·

The Perks of Being a Purple Cauliflower

MIDMORNING SNACK

· · · · · · · · · · · · · · · · · · ·

Lemongrass Cleansing Broth

LUNCH

· · · · · · · ·

Kale-ifornia Dreamin'

MIDAFTERNOON SNACK

· ·

Mi-So Healthy

DINNER

· · · · · · · · ·

And the Beet Goes On

SOUP TOPPINGS

Toppings are not required but they are so much fun! Almost like yin and yang, toppings can add texture, flavor, zing, and personality to any soup. Get creative!

+ Smooth on chunky

+ Bitter on savory

+ Salty on sweet

+ Crunchy on smooth

+ Sprouts—pea sprouts, daikon sprouts, and alfalfa sprouts are great for additional protein and beauty.

+ Seeds—roasted butternut squash and pumpkin seeds are divine on squash soups.

+ Herbs—fresh or roasted, herbs make a dramatic and flavorful topping.

+ Minced garlic, turmeric, or ginger

+ Herb-flavored oils are not just for beauty; they add another layer to your soup. I only use a teeny drop during the cleanse, so as not to slow the detox.

+ Mix and match: Use more than one topping—sprouts and seeds, for example. It's like adding a salad to your soup.

7

THE RECIPES

BLENDED SOUPS

•

CHUNKY SOUPS

•

BROTHS

•

RAW SOUPS

BLENDED SOUPS

Easy Peas-y

Cauliflower Me, Maybe?!

The Fennel Hurrah

I Can't Believe It's Butternut!

And the Beet Goes On

Don't Nettle for Less

Ba Ba Ba Boom

Kale-ifornia Dreamin'

I Yam Who I Yam

Sweet Coconut Thai Oh My!

With My Chick-a-Peas

That's Just Dandy!

Soak Up the Sunchoke

Don't Squash My Dreams

Cure for the Common Kohlrabi

Oh Snap!

The Perks of Being a Purple Cauliflower

Follow the Yellow Spice Road

The Truffle with Asparagus

You Say Tomato, I Say Yellow Tomato

I Don't Carrot All What They Say

I Gotcha Kabocha Covered

You're My Fava-rite!

I Heard It Through the Grapevine

I'm All Artichoke-d Up

EASY PEAS-Y

This soup is like summer in your mouth: energizing and full of exciting fresh flavors! It's a beautiful breakfast soup; it wakes you up and keeps you going. Peas are like baby powerhouses of nutrition, rich in protein and fiber; they contain many health protective properties, from cancer prevention (due to high amounts of coumestrol) and blood sugar regulation to even prevention of Alzheimer's, arthritis, and osteoporosis. I also love peas for their antiaging properties and help with erasing wrinkles. And the most unexpected benefit, peas make you feel good. Historically, peas were called the cure for the evil spirits, because of their magical ability to improve the mood. Coupled with mint, this soup becomes an addicting but healthy concoction.

Serves 4

+ Heat the oil in a soup pot over medium-high heat, add the onion, and sauté until soft.

+ Add the peas and celery and mix everything together.

+ Add the boiling filtered water, cover, and simmer over medium-low heat for 45 minutes.

+ Stir in the mint, add salt to taste, transfer everything to a Vitamix, and puree until a smooth and light consistency. Add more previously boiling water if the soup is too thick to achieve the light, brothy texture.

+ Taste and adjust the salt to your taste.

+ Serve hot or cold.

1 tablespoon coconut oil

1 large onion, chopped

1 pound green peas

2 celery stalks, cubed

5 cups boiling filtered water

Generous handful of mint, finely chopped

Himalayan pink salt

CAULIFLOWER ME, MAYBE?!

Cauliflower takes center stage in this beautiful white soup. This cruciferous plant is one of my all-time favorites! It's rich in the free-radical-fighting antioxidants, manganese, vitamin C, and carotenoids. And it's so tasty, I don't think you can ever go wrong with it. If white silk was a soup, this would be it. It is so elegant and satisfying, you will have a hard time convincing your friends that it's also good for you.

Serves 4-6

+ Cut the cauliflower florets off the central stalk and chop them roughly. Quarter the stalk and slice that, too.

+ Heat the oil in the soup pot over medium-high heat, add the onion and garlic, and sauté until the onion softens.

+ Add the cauliflower stalk and sauté for another 5 minutes. Add 3 cups of boiling filtered water, a little salt, and simmer for about 10 minutes.

+ Then add the cauliflower florets and more water to cover. Simmer for 30 minutes, or until the cauliflower is tender but not mushy.

+ Let the soup cool for 30 minutes, transfer everything to a Vitamix, and blend until smooth and silky. Add more boiling water if the soup is too thick. Add lemon juice and salt to taste.

+ Garnish with a wedge of lemon and caramelized onion.

+ Add a little kick with a pinch of cayenne, if you'd like.

1 large cauliflower head

2 tablespoons coconut oil

1 large yellow onion, chopped

3 garlic cloves, chopped

6 cups boiling filtered water

Juice of 1 lemon

Himalayan pink salt

Lemon wedges, for serving

Caramelized onion, for serving

Cayenne pepper, for garnish (optional)

TIP

You can add a zing to your white cauliflower soup with 1 teaspoon of turmeric, 1/2 teaspoon of ground fenugreek, and a 1/2-inch piece of fresh ginger, finely diced. Add them at the same time as you sauté the onion and garlic and watch your white soup turn yellow and bring in a whole new personality. Have fun with it and enjoy all the extra antioxidants.

THE FENNEL HURRAH

Fennel is so underrated in the United States. Come to think of it, so are leeks. And I'm not even talking about celery root, also known as celeriac. Every single time I buy it at the farmers market, I get asked what in the world I do with it. All three are the stars of this soup—a cleansing tour de force: a bone-building and antioxidant potion that is light, savory, and packed with disease-fighting powers. I truly believe it is a much healthier substitute to a daily multivitamin. It's that good!

Serves 4-6

+ Heat the coconut oil in a pot over medium-high heat and sauté the spring onions with the garlic and a pinch of Himalayan pink salt until the greens turn bright green, about 2 minutes.

+ Add the leeks and sauté until tender, another 2 to 3 minutes.

+ Add the fennel and sauté until tender, 3 minutes.

+ Stir in the celeriac, add more salt, mix all the veggies in the pot, and sauté for another few minutes.

+ Add the boiling filtered water, or enough to cover the veggies by about 2 inches.

+ Simmer over medium-low to low heat for 1 to 1 ½ hours, until all the veggies are very soft.

+ Transfer everything to a Vitamix and blend until smooth.

1 tablespoon coconut oil

1 bunch spring onions, cut

2 garlic cloves, bruised

Himalayan pink salt

2 leeks, cut into 2-inch chunks and then lengthwise

1 medium-size fennel bulb, quartered

1 medium-size celeriac, peeled and cubed

5 cups boiling filtered water

I CAN'T BELIEVE IT'S BUTTERNUT!

Soup for breakfast? If you are not sure about veggies first thing in the morning, this soup will change your mind. I've gone from "I'm not a fan a butternut" to craving this soup upon waking. And I'm not alone. I often get e-mails late at night from customers who just have to have it now. Butternut squash and red lentils are not only a match made in health heaven, this soup is delicious and has layers of flavor. Plus, it's packed with vitamins and nutrients such as vitamins B_6, C, folate, carotenoids, and lots of iron, essential for us vegans. This soup is great for breast health, bone, and immune strength, is a significant source of protein, and is soothing for digestion.

Serves 4-6

1 small butternut squash
(about 1 ½ pounds)

Himalayan pink salt

Olive oil, for drizzling

1 tablespoon coconut oil

1 small onion, chopped

½ teaspoon extra-virgin olive
oil

1 (2-inch) piece fresh ginger,
sliced

1 medium-size heirloom
tomato, quartered

½ cup sprouted red lentils

Boiling filtered water

+ Wash and halve the squash lengthwise, scraping out the seeds and pulp, reserving the seeds.

+ Preheat the oven to 375°F.

+ Cube the squash, season with salt, and drizzle with olive oil.

+ Arrange on a baking sheet and roast for 25 minutes, until the flesh is fork-tender.

+ Roast the reserved squash seeds on the same baking sheet alongside the squash, without oil.

+ Heat the coconut oil in a soup pot over medium-high heat, add the onion, and sauté until translucent. Add the ginger and sauté for another 3 minutes.

+ Add the roasted squash and sauté for another 3 minutes.

+ Add the tomato, sprouted lentils, and then enough boiling filtered water to cover. Simmer over medium-low to low heat for 30 minutes to an hour, until the lentils are very soft.

+ Let cool for another 30 minutes to absorb the flavors. Transfer everything to a Vitamix and blend until smooth.

AND THE BEET GOES ON

I grew up on Russian beet borscht, loaded with cabbage, beets, and big chunks of beef. The nostalgia for one of my favorite dishes from childhood pushed me to create an updated vegan version, with a modern flair. The result: a beety soup, packed with iron and flavonoids, lauded for their anticancer benefits and known to purify the body. And one of my favorite qualities of this soup: It reverses aging because of the high proportion of natural folic acid that contributes to the creation of new cells and, together with iron, production of red blood cells. It's good for hair, nails, and skin. You get it: It's the fountain of youth. To see a photo of this soup, go to page 108.

Serves 4-6

2 medium-size beets, scrubbed and quartered, tops reserved

Red pepper flakes

½ teaspoon extra-virgin olive oil

Himalayan pink salt

4 whole, unpeeled garlic cloves

1 tablespoon coconut oil

1 small sweet yellow onion, chopped

2 medium-size carrots, cut into 1-inch pieces

5 baby fingerling potatoes, or

2 medium-size red potatoes, cubed with skin on

1 medium-size tomato, cut into eighths, juice reserved

½ cup juice from fresh tomatoes

5 to 6 cups boiling filtered water

¼ cabbage head, trimmed and roughly sliced

Reserved beet tops, cut into thick ribbons

3 thyme sprigs

2 bay leaves

Fresh thyme, for serving (optional)

Crushed garlic, for serving (optional)

Coconut cream, for serving (optional)

+ Preheat the oven to 375°F.

+ Arrange the beets, tossed with red pepper flakes, olive oil, and salt, on a baking sheet.

+ On the same sheet, wrap the garlic cloves in foil to bake together.

+ Roast for 20 to 30 minutes, until the beets are soft.

+ Meanwhile, heat the coconut oil in a soup pot over medium-high heat, add the onion, and sauté until translucent.

+ Add the carrots and potatoes and sauté until al dente, another 3 minutes.

+ Mix in the tomato, roasted beets, and baked garlic.

+ Pour in the tomato juice with the boiling filtered water, and add the cabbage and beet tops.

+ Place the thyme sprigs and bay leaves in the pot and cover with a lid. Simmer over medium-low heat for 45 minutes to 1 hour.

+ Taste and adjust the salt as desired.

+ Remove from the heat; let stand to absorb and settle the flavors.

+ Remove the thyme sprigs and bay leaves from the pot, place everything in a Vitamix, and blend until smooth.

+ Serve with fresh thyme, crushed garlic, and/or a dollop of coconut cream.

NOTE

One of my favorite things with a bowl of borscht is a slice of freshly baked rustic rye bread with fresh raw garlic rubbed on its crust, plus a few grains of salt. Just don't do it during the cleanse.

And the Beet Goes On, page 106

DON'T NETTLE FOR LESS

I stumbled upon stinging nettles at the Santa Monica Farmers Market. The farmer sold me on this wonder plant, available only in the spring after a good rain and known for centuries to cure a long list of ailments, from arthritis and anemia to UTIs and even gout. Nettles are chock-full of vitamins A and C, iron, potassium, calcium, and manganese, and are short of miraculous in reducing inflammation in our body. The best confirmation that the soup works was the call from my daughter Madeline, who said it completely relieved her congestion.

Serves 4-6

+ Bring a large pot of water to a boil. Blanch the nettle tops for 2 minutes (make sure to wear protective gloves while handling the nettles, to avoid the sting).

+ Transfer the blanched nettles to a bowl of ice water to shock them. Strain. Discard any large stems.

+ Heat the coconut oil in a soup pot over medium-high heat, add the shallots and garlic, and sauté for 2 to 3 minutes, until fragrant.

+ Lower the heat to medium, add the fennel, celery, plus a pinch of salt, and sauté for 5 to 7 minutes, until they are soft but not browned.

+ Add the potatoes, thyme, and bay leaves to the pot, mix the veggies, and add boiling filtered water to cover. Bring to a simmer over medium-low heat and cook for 45 minutes, or until the potatoes are soft.

+ Roughly chop the blanched nettles, add to the pot, and simmer for another 15 minutes.

+ Remove the bay leaves and thyme from the pot, transfer everything to a Vitamix, and puree.

+ Add the lemon juice. Taste and adjust the seasoning.

1 bunch nettle tops

1 tablespoon coconut oil

2 shallots, chopped

3 garlic cloves, minced

1 fennel bulb, cut into eighths

4 celery stalks, chopped

Himalayan pink salt

3 medium-size white new potatoes, peeled and chopped

3 fresh thyme sprigs

2 bay leaves

5 cups boiling filtered water

Juice of 1/2 lemon

Caramelized garlic or shaved fennel, for garnish (optional)

BA BA BA BOOM

Eating my Grandma Freida's "eggplant caviar" (baba ghanoush) on a slice of dark bread is one of my favorite childhood memories. She'd roast eggplants and whip the flesh by hand, telling me that eggplant had medicinal properties and was "brain food." Eggplants pack a high volume of chlorogenic acid, which fights cancer; their skin has nasunin, a powerful antioxidant; and they marry beautifully with the flavors of tomatoes and my mom's favorite, roasted bell peppers.

Serves 4-6

6 medium-size on-the-vine tomatoes, halved

3 whole red bell peppers

Himalayan pink salt and freshly ground black pepper

3 tablespoons extra-virgin olive oil

1 whole garlic bulb

2 fresh thyme sprigs

1 medium-size eggplant (select it firm, plump, heavy, and dark purple-colored; make sure there are no bruises, scars, or discoloration)

1 red onion, cut into wedges

3 cups boiling filtered water

1 garlic clove, peeled and minced

+ Preheat the oven to 375°F. On a rimmed baking sheet, arrange the tomatoes, cut side down, and the bell peppers, and sprinkle with salt, pepper, and olive oil. On the same sheet, place the garlic bulb wrapped in a foil packet with a drizzle of olive oil and the thyme.

+ Place the baking sheet on the top rack and roast until tender, tossing halfway through if necessary, for about 20 minutes.

+ On another baking sheet, put the whole eggplant with a pinch of salt. Roast this baking sheet on the bottom rack until tender when pierced with a fork, 35 to 45 minutes, adding the red onion to the eggplant pan halfway through the baking time.

+ Peel and discard the tomato and bell pepper skins, reserve half of one bell pepper for garnish.

+ Place the peeled tomatoes and bell peppers in a Vitamix and puree. Extract the garlic flesh from the garlic bulb and add to the mixture. Transfer the mixture to the soup pot.

+ Puree the eggplant, stir into the mixture, and then thin with the boiling filtered water. Bring to a simmer over medium heat. Season with salt and pepper as desired.

+ Slice the reserved bell pepper into thin ribbons and toss them with salt and the minced fresh garlic for garnish.

KALE-IFORNIA DREAMIN'

I eat plenty of kale salads, but kale soup? The tough kale leaf is not the most scrumptious when cooked and I desperately wanted another take on the kale goodness. So, when I saw sorrel at my neighborhood farmers market, I did a happy dance. My mom used to make a sorrel soup (she called it Russian green borscht) that tasted lemony, tart, and oh so fresh! This soup is a surprising and totally new way to enjoy kale and all the health benefits that come with it. It's a great cleansing soup that leaves you satisfied, can lower cholesterol, supports your immune system, and is high in iron and vitamins C and K.

Serves 4-6

1 tablespoon coconut oil

1 medium-size onion, cut into eighths

1 medium-size potato, chopped

Himalayan pink salt and freshly ground black pepper

1 bunch Tuscan kale, roughly chopped (stems and leaves)

4 to 5 cups boiling filtered water

1 bunch (2 loosely packed cups) sorrel, chopped

+ Heat the coconut oil in a soup pot over medium-high heat, add the onion, and sauté until translucent.

+ Lower the heat to medium, add the potato, salt, and pepper and sauté for 3 minutes.

+ Add the kale and stir; watch the greens turn bright green.

+ Add the boiling filtered water, bring to a simmer, and cook until the potatoes are soft, about 30 minutes.

+ Add the sorrel and gently simmer for another 10 minutes.

+ Carefully ladle the soup into a Vitamix and blend until completely smooth.

+ Season with more salt, if needed, and serve immediately.

NOTE

If you can't find sorrel, substitute spinach and add lemon juice to amp the flavor. Add a pinch of cayenne for a kick.

Soupelina

I YAM WHO I YAM

The recipe for this soup was almost an accident. I picked up a few yams for roasting from one of my favorite local farmers. When I was arranging them on the baking sheet, I decided to sprinkle them with cardamom, for more nutritional benefits and its exquisite flavor. The gorgeous fragrance of spices was so inspiring that I decided to change my plan and make a soup instead. With just a few additions, I Yam Who I Yam became one of the most popular Soupelina flavors: velvety, rich, delicately sweet, but not heavy. Cardamom, a few other Ayurvedic spices, and fennel made it perfect for cleansing, as all ingredients work beautifully to detoxify the body.

Serves 4-6

4 medium-size yams, scrubbed and halved

2 tablespoons ground cardamom

¼ teaspoon fennel seeds

¼ teaspoon yellow mustard seeds

¼ teaspoon panch phoron

1 bunch spring onions

1 teaspoon ground turmeric

1 tablespoon coconut oil

1 medium-size fennel bulb, cut into eighths

Himalayan pink salt

Boiling filtered water

¼ teaspoon saffron

+ Preheat the oven to 400°F, arrange the yam halves on a baking sheet, sprinkle with 1 tablespoon of the cardamom powder, and roast for about 20 minutes, until soft.

+ Meanwhile, heat the coconut oil in a soup pot over medium heat, and add the mustard seeds, fennel seeds, and panch phoron. When the seeds begin to flutter, add the spring onions, the remaining tablespoon of cardamom, and the turmeric. Mix.

+ Stir in the fennel and a few pinches of salt, and sauté the mixture until the fennel is covered in spices.

+ Add the roasted yams and boiling filtered water to cover, add the saffron, and simmer for 30 to 45 minutes, until the fennel is very soft and the potato skins are separating from potato flesh.

+ Allow the soup to cool slightly to absorb the flavors, then puree in a Vitamix until it's perfectly smooth.

+ Pour the soup into a clean pot; taste and adjust the seasonings to your taste.

PANCH PHORON

You can find this delicious Indian five-spice blend at Whole Foods and other health food markets under Spicely Organic Spices brand. It might be fun to make your own with this easy recipe.

1 teaspoon cumin seeds

1 teaspoon brown mustard seeds

1 teaspoon fennel seeds

1 teaspoon nigella seeds (a.k.a. black cumin or kalonji)

1 ½ teaspoons fenugreek seeds

+ Simply combine all the seeds in a small cup.

SWEET COCONUT THAI OH MY!

The explosion of flavors in Thai cuisine is tantalizing and preparing Thai dishes is such a sensory experience for me. It's always a challenge, however, because the key to a truly Thai meal is the perfect balance of spicy, salty, sweet, sour, and bitter. It might take you a few attempts and many trips to your local Asian market to make this soup work, but don't give up. Instead of using sugar for the "sweet" part, I decided to include a sweet potato, packed with vitamin A and beta-carotene, a powerful antioxidant that offers protection against cancer, asthma, and heart disease. Galangal, a root in the ginger family with a more robust flavor, and kaffir lime leaves add delicate and exciting flavors to this soup.

Serves 4-6

1 tablespoon coconut oil

1 medium-size red onion, roughly chopped

1 (2-inch) knob fresh galangal or ginger

2 garlic cloves

1 teaspoon vegan Thai red curry paste
(more if you want the soup extra spicy)

1 lemongrass stalk, cut and pounded

2 kaffir lime leaves, torn

2 cups light coconut milk

2 pounds sweet potatoes, peeled and cut into
big chunks

5 cups boiling filtered water

1 cup fresh Thai basil

1 tablespoon Himalayan pink salt

Freshly squeezed lime juice, for serving
(optional)

+ Heat the oil in a soup pot over medium-high heat, add the onion, galangal, and garlic, and sauté until fragrant. Lower the heat to medium, add the red curry paste, lemongrass, kaffir lime leaves, and ½ cup of the coconut milk. Stir and cook for 3 minutes.

+ Add the sweet potatoes, mix them in, and then add the remaining 1½ cups of coconut milk. Cook over medium heat for 20 minutes.

+ When the mixture starts bubbling, add the boiling filtered water, Thai basil, and salt; lower the heat to a simmer, and cook until the potatoes are very soft, 30 to 45 minutes.

+ Remove from the heat and let stand for 30 minutes to absorb the flavors.

+ Remove the kaffir leaves and lemongrass from the mixture and transfer the rest to a Vita-mix. Puree until smooth and silky.

Soupelina

NOTE

Freshly squeezed lime juice is
the perfect finish for serving.

WITH MY CHICK-A-PEAS

According to Chinese medicine, garbanzo beans (a.k.a. chickpeas) regulate spleen and stomach functions and promote detoxification. Selenium, a mineral present in chickpeas, is the star here, preventing inflammation and folate, which plays a role in DNA synthesis blocks the formation of cancer cells from mutations in the DNA. It is no wonder that chickpea soup had to be a part of my soup lifestyle. The inspiration for this recipe came from Indian cuisine.

Serves 4-6

3 tablespoons extra-virgin olive oil

½ onion, diced

3 garlic cloves, minced

2 ½ cups cooked chickpeas with their cooking liquid

½ teaspoon curry powder

½ teaspoon ground coriander

½ teaspoon ground cumin

½ teaspoon garam masala

Juice of ½ lemon

4 cups boiling filtered water, plus more if needed

2 handfuls of spinach or cooked green peas

+ Heat the oil in a soup pot over medium-high heat, add the onion and garlic, and sauté until soft, about 3 minutes.

+ Add the chickpeas with the water they were cooked in, spices, and lemon juice, cover, and cook at a simmer for about 25 minutes.

+ Stir and continue to cook, adding boiling filtered water, until the chickpeas are soft.

+ Transfer to a Vitamix and blend until smooth, adding more boiling filtered water, if necessary, to thin it to your desired consistency.

+ Pour the soup into a clean pot and return to a simmer. Taste and adjust the spices to your taste.

+ Add the spinach, cover, and allow the spinach to wilt for 2 to 4 minutes. If using peas, add them and allow them to heat through.

Soupelina

THAT'S JUST DANDY!

Dandelion leaves, a digestive tonic, are a powerful antioxidant. I started with juicing them (talk about the liver flush!), then graduated to salads (just like the ancient Greeks and Romans), and eventually it was time to make a soup! After all, these bitter greens are the best for healing digestion issues; detoxifying the liver, kidneys, and gallbladder; and getting rid of bloating and water weight. Together, with cauliflower, you are getting an über-dose of vitamins (A, C, K) and amino acids (indole-3-carbinol and glutamine, among others) to guard your body from colds and flu as well as boost your immune system for cancer protection. This soup is also ideal for those who are retaining water after cancer treatments, especially the removal of the lymph nodes. And I love that it packs all the joys of spring into one pot.

Serves 4-6

+ Heat 1 tablespoon of the coconut oil in a soup pot over medium-high heat, add the roughly chopped onion and the garlic, and sauté until soft, about 3 minutes.

+ Lower the heat to medium, add the cauliflower, and cook, stirring, for about 5 minutes.

+ Add the boiling filtered water and cook at a simmer until the cauliflower is tender but not too soft, 15 to 20 minutes.

+ Add the dandelion greens and cover the pot. The greens will wilt within 1 to 2 minutes.

+ Remove from the heat and allow the soup to cool slightly to absorb the flavors.

+ Meanwhile, heat the remaining 1 tablespoon of oil in a pan and caramelize the finely diced onion.

+ Transfer the soup to a Vitamix and puree until it is thick and creamy.

+ Adjust the seasoning with salt and pepper to taste.

+ Garnish with the caramelized onion.

2 tablespoons coconut oil

2 medium-size onions (one roughly chopped, the other finely diced)

4 garlic cloves, minced

1 medium-size cauliflower head, chopped

4 to 5 cups boiling filtered water

1 bunch dandelion greens

Himalayan pink salt and freshly ground black pepper

SOAK UP THE SUNCHOKE

Sunchokes (a.k.a. Jerusalem artichokes), are nutty and sweet tasting. And even though they are a bit starchy, they are one of the finest sources of dietary fiber and have a respectable amount of iron (the highest among the edible roots). I love that sunchokes have antioxidant powers and together with chicory (a medicinal plant in ancient Egypt, prescribed by doctors, with proven anticancer properties), they create a potent cleansing soup, rich in potassium, magnesium, and inulin (soluble fiber that nourishes the gut's healthy flora and heals digestion).

Serves 4-6

3 garlic cloves, minced

1 leek, roughly chopped

2 chicory heads, or 1 curly endive lettuce, leaves separated

2 pounds sunchokes, scrubbed

1 teaspoon extra-virgin olive oil

Himalayan pink salt

2 tablespoons coconut oil

4 to 5 cups boiling filtered water

4 curly parsley sprigs, fried if desired (directions follow), for garnish

+ Preheat the oven to 375°F.

+ Mix the sunchokes with the olive oil and a pinch of salt and toss to coat. Arrange them on a baking sheet and roast for 35 minutes, until slightly tender.

+ Heat the coconut oil in a soup pot over medium-high heat, add the garlic, leek, and chicory, and sauté until soft, 3 to 4 minutes.

+ Mix in the sunchokes, stir, add more salt and the boiling filtered water, and bring to a simmer. Cook for about 30 minutes, until the sunchokes are very soft.

+ Remove from the heat and allow to cool slightly to absorb the flavors.

+ Transfer the mixture to a Vitamix and puree until smooth.

+ Taste and adjust the flavors with salt and seasonings.

+ Garnish with fresh or fried parsley.

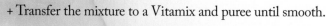

FRIED PARSLEY

+ Pour the depth of 2 inches of oil into a small pan and heat it over medium-high heat.

+ Test a sprig of parsley: It should sizzle but keep the color. If it turns brown, it's burnt.

+ Fry the parsley, carefully transfer to a paper towel, and pat dry to remove any excess oil.

DON'T SQUASH MY DREAMS

What's a girl to do when she craves Thai curry and the weather is hot? This soup recipe was born on a hot summer day after I got excited about fresh summer squash and zucchini at my farmers market. Zucchini have powerful antioxidant and anti-inflammatory properties, are high in vitamins A and C, offer cancer protection, are good for our eyes, and help lower cholesterol. Making a zucchini Thai soup became a goal. The soup is refreshing and light, with a smooth surface and beautiful, complex flavors underneath.

Serves 4-6

+ Heat the oil in a soup pot over medium-high heat, add the onion, galangal, and garlic, and sauté until fragrant.

+ Add the green curry paste, lemongrass, kaffir lime leaves, and ½ cup of the coconut milk. Stir and cook for 3 minutes.

+ Add the squash and potatoes, mix, then add the remaining 1½ cups of coconut milk. Cook over medium heat for 20 minutes.

+ When the mixture starts bubbling, add the boiling filtered water, Thai basil, and salt; lower the heat to a simmer; and cook until the potatoes are very soft, another 20 to 30 minutes.

+ Remove from the heat and let stand for 30 minutes to absorb the flavors.

+ Remove the kaffir leaves and lemongrass from the mixture and transfer the rest to a Vitamix. Puree until smooth and silky.

+ Freshly squeezed lime juice is the perfect finish for serving.

1 tablespoon coconut oil

1 medium-size yellow onion, roughly chopped

1 (2-inch) knob fresh galangal or ginger

2 garlic cloves

1 teaspoon vegan Thai green curry paste (more if you prefer soup extra spicy)

1 lemongrass stalk, cut and pounded

2 kaffir lime leaves, torn

2 cups coconut milk

2 pounds summer squash and/ or zucchini, cut into big chunks

2 medium-size gold potatoes, chopped

5 cups boiling filtered water

1 cup fresh Thai basil

1 tablespoon Himalayan pink salt

Freshly squeezed lime juice, for serving (optional)

CURE FOR THE COMMON KOHLRABI

I first spotted kohlrabi at my neighborhood farmers market and wondered what to do with this beautiful vegetable that looks more like a table centerpiece than a food. The farmer who was selling kohlrabi told me that she loves eating it raw or in a soup, and that it tastes like something between cabbage, radish, and broccoli. But most important, it is very good for respiratory problems and for thicker hair. How could I say no to that?! Like other cruciferous veggies, kohlrabi is rich in fiber, vitamin C, and potassium, and it boosts your immune system and energy. This soup is simple yet delicious and so very summery!

Serves 4-6

+ Heat the oil in a soup pot over medium-high heat, add the onion and garlic, and sauté until fragrant.

+ Add the kohlrabi, stir to coat, and sauté for 5 minutes.

+ Add the kale; watch it turn bright green.

+ Pour in the boiling filtered water to cover.

+ Cover, bring to a simmer, and cook until the veggies are soft but not mushy, 35 to 45 minutes.

+ Remove from the heat and allow to stand to absorb the flavors.

+ Transfer the mixture to a Vitamix and puree until smooth.

+ Taste and adjust the flavors with the salt and seasonings.

+ Garnish with radish sprouts or kale chips and serve hot.

1 tablespoon coconut oil

½ yellow onion, chopped

5 garlic cloves, finely chopped

3 kohlrabi bulbs, peeled and cut into wedges

1 bunch curly kale, stems and center discarded

5 cups or more boiling filtered water

Himalayan pink salt

Pinch of cayenne pepper, for serving

Radish sprouts or kale chips, for garnish (optional)

OH SNAP!

Once I fell in love with peas, I had to figure out another recipe. Playing in the kitchen is one of my favorite pastimes. Try it sometime. It's so fun adding different spices and veggies and watching them turn into a beautiful soup. There are no rules! I wanted to play on the sweet peas' flavors with mild zucchini and bitter watercress. Adding coriander was a gamble, but the soup came out bursting with flavors and I knew I had another favorite. This is a great blood-cleansing and anti-inflammatory soup. Oh snap!

Serves 4-6

2 tablespoons coconut oil

1 medium-size leek, white and tender green parts, cut into 3-inch pieces

1 garlic clove, minced

1 celery stalk, roughly chopped

3 medium-size zucchini, roughly chopped

½ teaspoon ground coriander

3 cups boiling filtered water

1 cup shelled peas

1 cup watercress, tough stems removed, plus more for garnish

Himalayan pink salt

Juice of ½ lemon

+ Heat the oil in a soup pot over medium-high heat, add the leek and garlic, and sauté until soft.

+ Add the celery, zucchini, and coriander, stir, and sauté for another 5 minutes.

+ Add enough boiling filtered water to cover the veggies, cover the pot, and simmer for 25 minutes.

+ Add the peas and watercress and cook for another 3 to 5 minutes, until the watercress is wilted and the peas are tender.

+ Remove from the heat and allow the flavors to absorb for 15 minutes.

+ Transfer the mixture to a Vitamix and puree until smooth.

+ Season with salt and lemon juice.

+ Serve hot or cold, garnished with watercress leaves.

NOTE

You can skip the zucchini and watercress if you don't have them on hand; just up the peas amount. You can also replace the watercress with arugula.

Soupelina

THE PERKS OF BEING A PURPLE CAULIFLOWER

Sometimes I wonder how people eat all the fake stuff when Mother Nature gives us such beautiful organic flavors and colors. Walking through the farmers market is inspiring and makes me feel alive. There is a reason for that: Pretty much everything I buy there has a direct impact on my body, mind, and spirit. Purple cauliflower is not just stunning looking; it also helps you look stunning. The purple color is a perk, a sign of flavonoid compounds called anthocyanins, instrumental in regulating blood sugar levels and body weight, and glucoraphanin, known for lowering your cancer risk.

Serves 4-6

+ Heat the oil in a soup pot over medium-high heat, add the celery and onion, and sauté until the onion is translucent.

+ Lower the heat to medium and add the cauliflower, reserving a few florets for garnish.

+ Add the potato and enough boiling filtered water to cover the veggies; cook until the cauliflower is al dente, 15 to 20 minutes.

+ Add the miso and garlic and cook for another few minutes.

+ Transfer to a Vitamix and puree until smooth.

+ Add the lime juice.

+ Taste and adjust the flavors with salt and seasonings.

+ Garnish with the reserved cauliflower florets.

1 tablespoon coconut oil

1 celery stalk, chopped

1 medium-size onion, sliced

1 head purple cauliflower, cut into large chunks

2 or 3 small potatoes, peeled and cubed

Boiling filtered water

1 tablespoon sweet white miso

2 garlic cloves, minced

Juice of 1 lime

Himalayan pink salt

NOTE

If you are not cleansing, serve the soup with 1/2 teaspoon of truffle oil for extra flavor pop.

FOLLOW THE YELLOW SPICE ROAD

I often think about my short trip to Morocco and dream about returning; the flavors and smells of this country's markets and the fragrance of Moroccan cuisine are unforgettable. Every time I make this yellow lentil soup, it mentally transports me to Morocco. I also love this soup because it is rich in fiber, folate, and iron. Lentils are great adrenal stimulants and are very beneficial to our heart and circulation.

Serves 4-6

+ Rinse and soak the lentils in water overnight. Drain the next day.

+ Heat the oil in a soup pot over medium heat, add the onion, and sauté until translucent.

+ Add the tomato, cumin, and red pepper flakes (if using) and stir.

+ Add the drained lentils and cover the mixture with the boiling filtered water.

+ Simmer for 30 minutes, or until the lentils are cooked.

+ Transfer everything to a Vitamix and puree until smooth.

+ Taste and adjust the flavors with salt, pepper, and lemon juice.

+ Garnish with the cilantro or parsley.

1 cup dried yellow lentils

2 tablespoons coconut oil

1 onion, sliced

1 tomato, grated

1 teaspoon ground cumin

1/2 teaspoon red pepper flakes (optional)

4 cups boiling filtered water

Himalayan pink salt and freshly ground black pepper

Juice of 1 lemon

Fresh cilantro or parsley, for garnish

NOTE

Lentils continue to expand after they are cooked. Make sure you are happy with the consistency. If you'd like the soup thinner, add more boiling filtered water.

THE TRUFFLE WITH ASPARAGUS

Asparagus looks like a spear, which I say is a symbol of its disease- and age-fighting powers. Rich in glutathione, a known detoxifying compound that helps break down carcinogens, asparagus is an anti-cancer weapon. Asparagus is also rich in B vitamins, folic acids, and plenty of antioxidants. I actually consider this soup to be my anti-aging go-to soup. This recipe is for the white asparagus soup with truffled oil like the elegant and delicate soup I once had in a fancy Parisian restaurant.

Serves 4-6

5 cups filtered water

2 bunches white asparagus

Juice of 1 lemon

Himalayan pink salt

1 tablespoon extra-virgin olive oil

1 large leek, white part only, roughly chopped

1 teaspoon truffle oil

TIP

Asparagus and iron pots are not friends and don't play together. Do not cook it in an iron pot because of the asparagus's reaction to iron.

+ Bring the filtered water to a boil over high heat.

+ Meanwhile, trim about 1 inch from the end of the asparagus, peel the skin from each spear, reserving the peels, and cut the spears in to 2-inch pieces. Gather the asparagus into two bundles and tie with kitchen string.

+ Add the reserved peels to the boiling water along with the lemon juice and salt.

+ Lower the heat to a simmer and add the asparagus bundles. Cook until tender, about 10 minutes. Be careful not to overcook.

+ Remove the asparagus and drain on paper towels. Strain the asparagus stock and place it back on the stove on the lowest heat, to remain hot.

+ Heat the oil in a soup pot, add the leek, and sauté until tender. Then pour in the asparagus stock, add the untied asparagus bundles, and simmer together for a few minutes.

+ Transfer the soup to a Vitamix and puree until velvety smooth.

+ Taste and adjust the flavor with salt and lemon juice.

+ Serve immediately with a drizzle of truffle oil.

Soupelina

YOU SAY TOMATO, I SAY YELLOW TOMATO

There is nothing I enjoy more than a simple red tomato salad, but I do worry about the acidity in tomatoes. So, when it comes to soup, packing it with red tomatoes to increase their anti-carcinogenic powers has been a no-no for me, because my tummy just wasn't able to handle that . . . until I discovered yellow tomatoes. Interestingly enough, the lycopene (responsible for those anticarcinogenic powers) that yellows have is different from the ones red tomatoes have, and the yellow tomato lycopene digests easier (and it's enhanced in the presence of oils!). Plus, when you compare red and yellow tomatoes, yellow ones win with the amount of iron and minerals they provide. Make sure the tomatoes you buy are organic and local, and hopefully from a neighborhood farmers market. They will most likely be smaller than the ones you will find in stores, but I promise, you will taste the difference in juiciness and flavor.

Serves 4

2 tablespoons extra-virgin olive oil, plus more if needed for blending

1 medium-size onion, minced

3 garlic cloves, peeled and sliced

6 large yellow tomatoes, cored and quartered

4 cups boiling filtered water

4 fresh basil leaves

Himalayan pink salt and freshly ground black pepper

+ Heat the oil in a soup pot over medium heat, add the onion and garlic, and sauté until translucent.

+ Add the tomatoes and cook for 5 minutes.

+ Pour in the boiling filtered water, add the basil, and stir.

+ Season with salt and pepper, then transfer the mixture to a Vitamix and puree until smooth. You can add more olive oil for a smoother consistency.

NOTE

Try Green Tomato Tartare as garnish to make a fancy soup. The color-play alone is worth it.

Soupelina

GREEN TOMATO TARTARE

2 green heirloom tomatoes

½ shallot, minced

1 garlic clove, minced

Leaves from 1 lemon thyme sprig

Himalayan pink salt

+ Peel and halve the tomatoes.

+ Squeeze out the juice and seeds, reserving the juice.

+ Cube the tomatoes into tiny pieces. Drain thoroughly or else they won't hold.

+ In a bowl, mix the tomatoes with the shallot, garlic, lemon thyme, and salt to taste.

+ To serve, place the tartare into a ring mold and press with paper towel to release some of
  the juice. Unmold the tartare onto bowls. You can also shape the tartare by hand.

I DON'T CARROT ALL WHAT THEY SAY

I have to confess; cooked carrots are not my faves and I mostly enjoy them raw. But I changed my mind last year when I ate a roasted carrot salad in Marais, the Jewish quarter of Paris. It was so perfectly seasoned with spices that I kept craving it long after the trip. And, naturally, I decided to see how it would be as a soup, especially since I read a study that showed cooking carrots boosts their nutritional content. The inspired soup turned out beautifully and every time I have a bowl of this spicy wonder, I know I'm being kind to myself. Of course, it helps to know that science is on my side and that besides its flavor, carrot soup is a great preventative for chronic diseases, is super cleansing, has anti-inflammatory properties, and is known to purify and revitalize the blood.

Serves 4

+ Heat the oil in a soup pot over medium-high heat, add the onion, and sauté until translucent.

+ Add the carrots and spices, and mix everything together so the mixture is coated with spices. (Go easy on harissa if too spicy is not your speed; this spice is hot!)

+ Add the boiling filtered water and simmer for about 45 minutes, until carrots are al dente.

+ Leave for 30 minutes for the flavors to mature.

+ Transfer to a Vitamix and blend until smooth, adding salt to taste.

+ Add the apple cider vinegar to the soup and swirl. Taste and add more, if desired.

+ Throw in the fresh arugula for color and bite.

2 tablespoons coconut oil

1 onion, chopped

1 pound carrots, peeled, roughly chopped

¼ teaspoon harissa

½ teaspoon ground cumin

¼ teaspoon caraway seeds, freshly ground

4 to 5 cups boiling filtered water

1 tablespoon apple cider vinegar

1 ½ cups arugula

I GOTCHA KABOCHA COVERED

The unusual pairing of kabocha squash with Middle Eastern spices is just another play on ingredients I so enjoy. This soup is a Middle Eastern feast: filling, flavorful, and exciting. It makes you think of your own trips to the Middle East or dream of going there. Packed with beta-carotene that converts into vitamin A, the soup is great for immunity, white blood cells, and eye health, and it keeps your hair and skin shiny and healthy.

Serves 4-6

1 medium-size (2 ½-pound) kabocha squash, cut into wedges

Himalayan pink salt and freshly ground black pepper

½ teaspoon extra-virgin olive oil

1 tablespoon coconut oil

1 medium-size red onion, cut into wedges

1 tablespoon za'atar (see page 141), plus a pinch for garnish

2 tablespoons tahini

Juice of 1 lemon

1 garlic clove, minced

4 to 5 cups boiling filtered water

1 tablespoon fresh flat-leaf parsley, for garnish

+ Preheat the oven to 375°F.

+ Wash and halve the kabocha, scraping out the seeds and pulp.

+ Cube the kabocha, season with salt and pepper, and drizzle with the olive oil.

+ Arrange on a baking sheet and roast for 25 minutes, or until the flesh is fork-tender.

+ Heat the coconut oil in a soup pot over medium-high heat, add the onion, and sauté until translucent.

+ Add the za'atar, tahini, lemon juice, garlic, and salt to create a pasty mixture with the sautéed onion. Add a little boiling filtered water to thin, if necessary.

+ Add the roasted kabocha and boiling filtered water.

+ Simmer for 30 minutes, then remove from the heat.

+ Let cool for 30 minutes to absorb the flavors.

+ Transfer everything to a Vitamix and blend until smooth.

+ Serve hot, with a pinch of za'atar to bring the flavors together.

+ Garnish with parsley, if desired.

Soupelina

ZA'ATAR

+ Combine 1 tablespoon of minced dried thyme,
  1 tablespoon of toasted sesame seeds, 1 tablespoon
  of ground sumac, 1 tablespoon of ground marjoram,
  and 1½ teaspoons of Himalayan pink salt.

+ Store in a glass jar for up to six months.

YOU'RE MY FAVA-RITE!

The only problem with fava beans is that they are only available in the springtime. Of course, you can buy them frozen year-round, but I prefer them fresh from the pod even though it is a pain shelling them and then removing the beans from their skins. Like other legumes, they are high in protein: Favas have 25 grams in only 3 ounces! I love favas sautéed with garlic, I love them simmered with parsley and lemon juice and I love them in soups. The high content of fiber in favas is great for the health of our intestines and colon. Combining them with romaine lettuce and leeks makes this soup rich in vitamin C for a healthy immune system, skin, bones, and teeth.

Serves 4-6

1 tablespoon coconut oil

2 garlic cloves, minced

1 medium-size leek, roughly chopped

1 medium-size onion, chopped

1 head romaine lettuce, ribs removed and reserved, leaves roughly torn

1 large celery stalk, roughly chopped

1 tablespoon chopped fresh dill

Himalayan pink salt

2 cups double-shelled fava beans

4 cups boiling filtered water

1 tablespoon freshly squeezed lemon juice

Freshly ground black pepper

Fresh dill leaves, for garnish

+ Heat the oil in a soup pot over medium-high heat, add the garlic, leek, and onion, and sauté until soft.

+ Add the lettuce ribs, celery, and dill; stir, and cook for 10 minutes.

+ Add a few pinches of salt.

+ Add the fava beans, reserving a few for garnish, and then immediately add the boiling filtered water; cook at a simmer for about 10 minutes, until the beans are tender.

+ Add the lettuce leaves and cover the pot. The greens will wilt within 1 to 2 minutes.

+ Ladle the soup into a Vitamix and puree until smooth.

+ Transfer to a clean pot, add the lemon juice, and season with salt to taste.

+ Garnish with the reserved beans and dill leaves.

Soupelina

HOW TO SHELL AND PREPARE FAVA BEANS

I find fava beans to be prudish and mysterious. The tall, meaty beans
are also deceptive and if you are not familiar with them, it takes a few
attempts to get to know them well. Plan on buying more than you think
you need because it takes quite a few bean pods to get 2 cups for the
recipe. Select pods that are smooth and rich green in color. If the beans
feel bulgy, that means they are old and will taste bitter. Here is a fava
undressing, step by step.

+ "Unzip" the seam of the bean pod by running a finger up the seam and pulling off the top stem. There are four or five beans per pod.

+ Open the pod and remove the beans; even inside, they will be "dressed" in an outer waxy coat.

+ Blanch the beans in boiling water for just 30 seconds and then immediately transfer to an ice bath to stop the cooking process.

+ When you squeeze each bean now, the waxy coat should just slip off.

+ You are now ready to cook your fava-rite soup!

IMPORTANT

Fava beans are high in tyramine, an amino acid that regulates blood pressure, which is normally very good for us. However, people who take antidepressants and other MAO (monoamine oxidase) inhibitors should not eat this soup. MAO medications cause tyramine to not break down and instead, to build up in the blood, leading to increased blood pressure and other symptoms.

I HEARD IT THROUGH THE GRAPEVINE

I grew up picking grapes from my bedroom window. I loved munching on young leaves as well; they tasted lemony and so fresh. Since I turn everything into soup, I decided to play with grape leaves. And why not? They are great for blood and energy deficiency, regulate blood sugar, and apparently relieve menopausal symptoms, such as night sweats. They are rich in vitamins A, B_6, C, E, and K, as well as calcium, and magnesium, and they are a surprising source of healthy omega-3 fatty acids! Fresh grape leaves contain about 2 percent fat and are on the list of plant-based foods with omega-3s, such as flax and chia seeds. Combined with fennel, this soup is another powerful antioxidant potion and a great soup for bone, muscle, and nerve health.

Serves 4-6

2 tablespoons extra-virgin olive oil

1 medium-size onion, chopped

2 garlic cloves, minced

Himalayan pink salt and freshly ground black pepper

1 fennel bulb, quartered

2 medium-size white potatoes, chopped

15 grape leaves (fresh or in brine), chopped

½ cup fresh mint leaves

4 to 5 cups boiling filtered water

Juice of 2 lemons

Dehydrated mint or grape leaves, for garnish

+ Heat the olive oil in a soup pot over medium-high heat, add the onion and garlic, and sauté until tender, about 5 minutes.

+ Stir in a little salt and pepper.

+ Add the fennel and sauté for another 3 minutes, until tender.

+ Add the potatoes and sauté for 3 minutes, until tender.

+ Stir in the grape leaves, mint, and boiling filtered water.

+ Simmer until the potatoes and grape leaves are very soft, 30 to 45 minutes.

+ Add more salt and pepper to taste.

+ Transfer everything to a Vitamix and blend until smooth.

+ Add the lemon juice. Serve hot.

NOTE

Unless you live near a vineyard, finding grape leaves could be tricky. But do not despair. Find a close-by Middle Eastern or Eastern European store and if it doesn't have fresh ones, most likely it will sell grape leaves preserved in brine. Another trick is to ask your local fruit farmers who sell grapes. That's what I do! They are always happy to bring you the grape leaves.

I'M ALL ARTICHOKE-D UP

Spiky artichokes are not only pretty but a delicious treat as well. This is the type of vegetable I call a conversation piece . . . and there is a lot to talk about! The member of the thistle family is a powerful liver cleanser! It contains a number of phytonutrients (apigenin, cynarin, silymarin, and luteolin) that have diuretic properties, detoxify the liver, boost gall bladder function, and improve bile flow. Artichokes are even used in Traditional Chinese Medicine as a remedy for water retention and liver ailments; they also aid digestion and help people who experience stomach acidity. Combined with garlic, thyme, and a blend of potent herbs and spices, this soup is one of the best cleansing potions you can have.

Serves 4-6

+ Heat the oil in a soup pot over medium-high heat, add the leeks and garlic, and sauté for 5 minutes, or until the leeks are translucent.

+ Add the artichoke hearts, potatoes, thyme, and boiling filtered water. Simmer over medium-low heat until the leeks and artichoke hearts are soft, 30 to 45 minutes.

+ Remove the thyme sprigs and strip the remaining leaves into the pot.

+ Transfer to a Vitamix and blend until silky.

+ Add the lemon juice to the soup.

+ Serve with a swirl of green harissa for extra nutritional and medicinal benefits, plus a dose of oomph.

1 tablespoon extra-virgin olive oil

2 medium-size leeks, roughly chopped

3 garlic cloves

2 cups fresh or frozen artichoke hearts (thaw if frozen)

2 medium-size potatoes, cubed

5 thyme sprigs

4 cups boiling filtered water

Juice of ½ lemon

Green Harissa Topping, for serving (recipe follows)

GREEN HARISSA TOPPING

½ cup fresh parsley

½ cup fresh cilantro

Juice of 1 lemon

½ cup extra-virgin olive oil

1 serrano chile

½ teaspoon fennel seeds

½ teaspoon ground cumin

½ teaspoon ground
 coriander

Himalayan pink salt

+ Combine all the ingredients in a food processor and pulse until coarsely chopped.

+ This will keep for up to a week stored in the fridge.

CHUNKY SOUPS

Lentil Me Entertain You

Make 'Shroom for Me

It's Chili and It's Hot

A-Mung the Stars

I'll Be Bok, Choy!

Beet the Heat

Oh Dhal-ing!

Guys and Dhals

Gone with the Watercress

Mi-So Healthy

What's the Hurry, Melon Curry?

LENTIL ME ENTERTAIN YOU

It all started with the lentil soup. Can you believe I hadn't tried lentils until I started eating vegan? Not sure what to expect, I wanted to throw all the "anticancer" ingredients I knew of into one dish. I read that lentils protect our nervous system and improve mood, and I so needed that! Shiitake mushrooms, turmeric, cumin, carrots, and celery were helping to protect my immune system and to slow (and even stop) cancer growth. And I really wanted the soup to taste good. What happened in the pot was short of miraculous: my soup turned into a satisfying potion busting with flavors: clean, fresh, and well balanced. After one bowl I felt healthier.

Serves 4-6

1 cup dried small green lentils

Boiling water, enough to cover mushrooms

1 cup sliced, dried organic shiitake mushrooms, washed

1 tablespoon extra-virgin olive oil

4 spring onions, cut diagonally into thin pieces

Himalayan pink salt

1 teaspoon ground turmeric

1 teaspoon ground cumin

2 medium-size carrots, cubed

2 celery stalks, cubed

2 bay leaves

Cayenne pepper, for serving

+ Wash the lentils and soak them overnight with warm water.

+ Pour boiling water over the washed dried shiitake mushrooms and leave them to soak for at least 30 minutes. Strain the mushrooms through a fine-mesh strainer into a clean container. Reserve the soaking water.

+ Bring the reserved mushroom water to a boil. Add the lentils and cook over medium heat for about 20 minutes.

+ Meanwhile, heat the oil in a skillet over medium-low heat, add the onions, and sauté them for 1 minute, until they turn bright green.

+ Add the mushrooms and a little salt and sauté for another 2 minutes.

+ Add the turmeric and cumin and sauté for an additional 2 minutes, until the onions and mushrooms are coated with the spices.

+ While the lentils are cooking, add the mushroom mixture, plus the carrots, celery, and bay leaves, to the pot and stir. Cover and simmer for 15 minutes, until the lentils, mushrooms, and veggies are al dente.

+ Taste and adjust the salt to your liking. Serve with a kick of cayenne.

MAKE 'SHROOM FOR ME

People who know me get a fill of my stories of how, as a teenager, I foraged for mushrooms in the Russian forests. They joke that I'm like a truffle dog because I can tell which mushroom is good by its smell and look. Mushrooms' deep, rich, earthy flavor is insanely satisfying, all due to umami, the elusive fifth taste, that they have been blessed with. They are naturally low in sodium and have been studied for their health-promoting benefits, including immune support, high vitamin D levels, and even anticancer properties. In fact, Chinese Medicine considers shiitake mushrooms both a delicacy and a medicinal mushroom. This soup is an ode to mushrooms, of sorts. I love this soup chunky, but if you are like my daughter, who loves pureed soups, blend it for your own creamless "cream of mushroom" soup.

Serves 4-6

Boiling water, enough to cover mushrooms

2 cups dried organic sliced shiitake
   mushrooms, washed

1 whole garlic bulb

2 tablespoons organic coconut oil

2 large leeks, white part only, sliced thinly
   into circles

1 cup tiny organic cremini mushrooms, scrubbed,
   halved or quartered, depending on size

1 cup small organic white button mushrooms,
   scrubbed, halved or quartered

10 baby fingerling potatoes, halved or
   quartered, depending on size

4 threads saffron

1 bay leaf

3 fresh thyme sprigs

Himalayan pink salt and freshly ground black
   pepper

1 ½ teaspoons fresh parsley, chopped, for
   garnish

+ Pour boiling water over the washed dried shiitake mushrooms and leave them to soak for at least 30 minutes.

+ Preheat the oven to 350°F, place the garlic on a small baking sheet, and bake, uncovered, for 45 minutes. Set aside to let cool. Then squeeze the garlic cloves into a small bowl, discard the peels, and mash the pulp into a paste.

+ Drain the soaked shiitakes, reserving the water. Wash the mushrooms carefully, getting rid of all the grit. Strain the soaking water through a paper filter and set aside.

+ Meantime, heat the oil in a soup pot, add the leeks, and sauté for 2 minutes.

+ Add all the mushrooms and sweat them until they are reduced in size, 3 to 5 minutes.

+ Add the potatoes, reserved mushroom water, garlic paste, saffron, bay leaf, thyme, and salt and pepper to taste.

+ Simmer over medium-low heat for 30 to 45 minutes, until the potatoes are tender and the soup is golden-brown. Let stand for about 30 minutes to absorb the flavors. Or make the soup at night and leave overnight to absorb flavors.

+ Serve hot, garnished with the parsley.

NOTE

When chanterelles and porcinis are in season, go ahead and add them to the soup. Or sauté them in a little bit of oil and use as a garnish for the pureed version. At home, I use all mushrooms I can get my hands on: shimeji, king trumpets, maitake, and oyster.

Make 'Shroom for Me, page 154

It's Chili and It's Hot, page 158

IT'S CHILI AND IT'S HOT

This soup is the favorite of everyone who tries it, vegan or not. The hearty chili has more protein than a steak, and it's all plant-based! It's also great for regulating blood sugar levels and disarming free radicals; it's full of fiber, flavonoids, and molybdenum, a trace mineral that breaks down and detoxifies sulfites. And to make my chili extra special, I decided to forgo the traditional rice and include quinoa, super famous for anti-inflammatory phytonutrients, not to mention the impressive list of vitamins B_1, B_2, B_3, B_6, and B_9, plus such minerals as potassium, copper, zinc, and magnesium. Each bowl actually has disease-fighting powers and is bursting with flavor! To see a photo of this soup, go to page 157.

Serves 6

½ cup red quinoa, soaked overnight

½ cup white quinoa, soaked overnight

Extra-virgin olive oil

1 onion, chopped

2 garlic cloves, minced

1 jalapeño pepper, diced

1 medium-size carrot, peeled and chopped

2 celery stalks, chopped

1 yellow bell pepper, chopped

1 red bell pepper, chopped

1 orange bell pepper, chopped

1 zucchini, chopped

1 cup black beans, soaked overnight and cooked

1 cup kidney beans, soaked overnight and cooked

2 diced tomatoes with juice

1 cup freshly pressed tomato juice

1 tablespoon ground cumin

Handful of fresh oregano leaves, or ½ tablespoon dried

Himalayan pink salt and freshly ground black pepper

1 tablespoon chili powder

2 to 3 cups boiling filtered water

Sliced avocado, fresh cilantro sprigs, and chopped onion, for garnish

+ In a medium-size saucepan, boil 2 cups of water, add the quinoa, lower the heat to a simmer, and cook until the water is absorbed, about 20 minutes. Set aside.

+ Heat a little olive oil in a large soup pot over medium heat, add the onion, and sauté until translucent, about 5 minutes.

+ Stir in the garlic, jalapeño, carrot, celery, peppers, and zucchini and cook until the veggies are tender, about 10 minutes.

+ Add all the beans, tomatoes, and tomato juice, along with the cumin, oregano, salt, and black pepper. Taste before slowly adding chili powder to your desired spiciness.

+ Add the quinoa and boiling filtered water and simmer for 30 minutes.

+ Keep stirring and adding spices and salt until you are happy with the taste.

+ Garnish with avocado slices, cilantro, and onion.

A-MUNG THE STARS

You won't know what you've been missing until you eat your first bowl of mung bean soup. Mung beans are teeny green or yellow legumes cherished in Indian cuisine. Their delicate flavor, high protein content, and holistic qualities made them a staple in my diet. Mung beans have been used as powerful detoxifier in Asian cuisines and medicine for centuries. This soup is loaded with antioxidant properties, can fight disease, and protect your body, and is perfect for restoring balance if you are healing, fatigued, or have digestive issues. One of my favorite health benefits of mung bean soup is that it helps with irritability and headaches.

Serves 4-6

½ cup dried green mung beans

3 cardamom pods

3 tablespoons extra-virgin olive oil

1 onion, chopped

1 small knob ginger, minced

3 garlic cloves, minced

¼ teaspoon freshly ground black pepper

1 heaping teaspoon ground turmeric

1 heaping teaspoon ground cumin

¼ teaspoon crushed red chiles

½ teaspoon ground coriander

Himalayan pink salt

5 cups boiling filtered water

3 to 4 cups chopped veggies (carrots, celery, zucchini, broccoli, cauliflower, etc.)

½ cup organic brown basmati rice

Red pepper flakes, for garnish (optional)

+ Wash the mung beans and rinse them several times. Soak the beans overnight.

+ Crack the cardamom pods open and scrape out the seeds. Crush the seeds in a mortar and pestle.

+ Dry roast the cardamom seeds in a dry skillet until they flutter and release their aroma and essential oils.

+ Heat the oil in a soup pot over medium heat, add the onions, ginger, garlic, black pepper, spices, including cardamom seeds and salt. Sauté until the mixture becomes pasty.

+ Add the mung beans and boiling filtered water, and cook over medium heat until the beans have boiled into a gravylike liquid, 60 minutes to 1 hour 30 minutes.

+ Add the veggies and rice, lower the heat to a simmer, and cook for another 20 minutes.

+ Taste and adjust the salt and spices to your liking.

+ Serve hot. Add red pepper flakes for spiciness, if desired.

I'LL BE BOK, CHOY!

One of my favorite things while traveling through Asia is the heaping bowls of soups I could get just about anywhere. That's the Asian version of fast food. The bowls are always quick and it's a joy to sit down and enjoy the flavors of nutritious fresh veggies. I set out to re-create the flavors I so love with all the veggies and roots I have to have in my diet. And I'll Be Bok, Choy! was born! Bok choy, the star of this soup, is a superhero with antioxidant powers as well as vitamins A, C, and K. Together with daikon, carrots, onions, and shiitakes, this soup will protect your health any season.

Serves 6

+ Heat the olive oil and sesame oil together in a soup pot over medium heat.

+ Add the onion and garlic. Sauté, stirring occasionally, with a little salt, until soft and golden, about 15 minutes.

+ Add the mushrooms, ginger, daikon, and carrot and sauté together for another 5 minutes.

+ Pour in the boiling filtered water, add the tamari, and cook until the mixture reaches a soft boil.

+ Lower the heat to a simmer, add the bok choy, cover, and simmer for 5 minutes.

+ Remove from the heat, adjust the flavors, and serve.

+ For a spicy flavor, add red pepper flakes or serrano chile.

1 tablespoon olive oil

1 teaspoon sesame oil

Himalayan pink salt

1 medium-size yellow onion, thinly sliced

2 garlic cloves, thinly sliced

2 cups fresh shiitake mushrooms, sliced

1 1/2 teaspoons fresh ginger, grated

1 cup julienned daikon

1 cup julienned carrot

8 cups boiling filtered water

1/4 cup tamari

3 baby bok choy, halved

Red pepper flakes or serrano chile, for servings (optional)

BEET THE HEAT

Here is a spectacular spin on all things fermented. I'm so into everything pickled that I had to create a soup combining all of the things I can't live without, including my own home-pickled veggies (recipe follows). If you haven't gotten on the DIY fermented food kick yet, you can pick up all the ingredients at a health foods market. If you would like to experiment, join me on a quick fermented journey. I promise you, it's easy and the health benefits are enormous. This soup is an immunity- and health-boosting potion, full of friendly intestinal bacteria, lactobacilli, and enzymes that heal digestion, strengthen the gut, and help our body absorb all the nutrients we need. If you eat this soup year-round, you will never get a cold.

Serves 4

4 cups raw organic beet kombucha (I like Health-Ade brand) or Beet Kvass (page 188)

2 cups sauerkraut (recipe follows)

2 unpasteurized pickles, sliced into semicircles

5 fresh or fermented radishes, sliced into semicircles

2 fresh or fermented carrots, sliced into circles

10 assorted baby fingerling potatoes, halved or quartered depending on size, boiled and chilled

½ teaspoon Himalayan pink salt

1 tablespoon apple cider vinegar

Cayenne pepper

Fresh dill or parsley, for garnish

+ Combine all the ingredients, except the dill, in a bowl.

+ Taste and adjust the salt, cayenne, and apple cider vinegar.

+ Garnish with fresh dill or parsley and serve chilled.

Soupelina

SAUERKRAUT

½ cabbage head, finely chopped

1 garlic clove, chopped

1 tablespoon Himalayan pink salt

1 tablespoon dried dill

+ Place the cabbage and garlic in a large bowl.

+ Mix in the salt and dill, and massage the cabbage mixture with your hands for 5 minutes.

+ Place a plate on top of the cabbage mixture and put a weight on top (a few clean marbles or stones). Place in a cool, dry location.

+ Over the next day, press down on the cabbage mixture so it releases its liquid and becomes limp.

+ Check after 2 days; allow to ferment for 3 to 4 days away from direct sunlight. Keep pressing down if the cabbage mixture floats above the liquid. When the sauerkraut tastes good to you, place in the fridge.

PICKLED VEGGIES

Whole Persian cucumbers, radishes, and carrots

1 tablespoon mustard seeds

4 garlic cloves, smashed

3 celery stalks, roughly chopped

2 tablespoons sea salt

1 tablespoon coconut sugar

1 tablespoon apple cider vinegar

Several whole black peppercorns

Red pepper flakes

Whole cloves

Plenty of fresh dill leaves and stems

+ Combine everything in a large jar.

+ Pour in water to cover, cover the jar with cheesecloth, and store in a cool, dry area. Allow to ferment for 2 to 3 days, then transfer to the fridge.

OH DHAL-ING!

Dhal is the perfect winter soup. But because it is so nutritious, easy to make, and has a ton of flavor, it's become a year-round comfort food for me. Besides the goodness and high protein of red lentils, the health benefits come from all the spices that not only make this soup special and fragrant, but protect your body from diseases. Good for acid reflux and blood circulation, dhal also helps reduce blood sugar levels, especially regulating the blood sugar spikes after a meal, controls hypertension, prevents anemia, and lowers cholesterol. Once you get a hang of it, you can add any veggies in season, such as spinach, fresh peas, or broccolini.

Serves 4-6

+ Drop the mustard seeds, cumin seeds, coriander seeds, and nigella seeds into a dry skillet and dry roast for a couple of minutes until the seeds pop, releasing their essential oils and aromas.

+ Heat the oil in a large pot over medium heat and transfer the seeds to the pot.

+ Immediately add the onion and jalapeño and sauté together with the seeds until the onion and jalapeño are soft and translucent.

+ Mix in the garlic and ginger and a little salt.

+ Add the tomato and cook for a few minutes longer. Stir throughout the process and adjust the heat if needed so your ingredients don't burn.

+ Add all the spices, mix, and watch them absorb all the liquid in the pot.

+ Add the lentils and boiling filtered water. Cook over medium heat, covered, stirring occasionally, until the lentils are very soft and fall completely apart, 30 to 45 minutes.

+ Mash with a potato masher for smooth, creamy consistency. If you like texture, mash only the cooked garlic with a fork and mix.

1 teaspoon cumin seeds

1 teaspoon mustard seeds

1 teaspoon coriander seeds

½ teaspoon nigella seeds

3 tablespoons coconut oil

1 large onion, diced

1 jalapeño pepper, sliced

5 garlic cloves, minced

1 small knob fresh ginger, minced

Himalayan pink salt

1 large tomato, diced

1 teaspoon ground turmeric

1 teaspoon garam masala

1 teaspoon ground cumin

1 teaspoon curry powder

1 cup washed and drained dried red lentils

5 cups boiling filtered water

GUYS AND DHALS

This recipe comes from Martha Soffer, my favorite Ayurvedic therapist and chef, and a beautiful soul. Martha serves this dhal soup at her Surya Spa, when people come to her to heal, cleanse, and rejuvenate. This delicious soup is made of split yellow mung beans, a rich source of plant-based protein, iron, and potassium. Martha stresses to only use organic dhal—there's a lot of surface area in a collection of small beans, and believe it or not, some sellers artificially dye their mung! For the dhal spices, she recommends this Vata-pacifying (or calming) mixture, which also helps with digestion and is balancing to all three doshas.

Serves 4

1 cup dried yellow dhal, washed and scrubbed with your hands

6 cups filtered water

2 teaspoons Himalayan pink salt

½ teaspoon ground turmeric

½ teaspoon ground cumin

½ teaspoon ground coriander

½ teaspoon ground fennel

1 teaspoon coconut oil

1 cup fresh cilantro

Black lava salt, for garnish

Pinch of black sesame seeds, for garnish

+ In a soup pot, stir the dhal into the water and bring to a soft boil.

+ Remove any foam from the top as it rises; stir, cover, lower the heat, and simmer for 30 minutes.

+ Combine the salt and all the spices in a skillet and sauté in a little coconut oil to properly activate the spices and bring out their innate healing properties.

+ Add the fresh cilantro to the cooked spices, and let that sauté as well.

+ Add the spice mixture to the dhal, putting a little water in the pan to get everything out.

+ Taste and add more salt, if needed.

+ Garnish with a little black lava salt and black sesame seeds, for a balancing and satisfying meal.

GONE WITH THE WATERCRESS

I've been looking to bring watercress into my diet for a while, but for some reason, I shied away from its bitter, peppery flavor. Until I read studies that it has significant levels of glucosinolate compounds, which means major anticancer benefits. Having these compounds in your body appears to help inhibit breast, lung, colon, and prostate cancers. When I remembered the delicious roasted chickpeas and carrots dish I had in Capetown, spiced with the intense North African blend called ras el hanout, I decided to play with the flavors. The sweetness of chickpeas totally worked with the bitterness of watercress, and the flavors seriously transported me to another continent. Not to mention the soup's health benefits: It's an antidote to fatigue, and great for detoxifying your body, healing your respiratory and digestive systems, and protecting against free radicals.

Serves 4

+ Preheat the oven to 350°F.

+ Combine the carrots and cooked chickpeas with the ras el hanout and a sprinkle of olive oil, and arrange on a baking sheet lined with parchment paper. Roast for 15 to 20 minutes, until al dente. Reserve half of the spiced chickpeas and set aside.

+ Meanwhile, heat the oil in a soup pot over medium heat, add the onion and ginger, and sauté until the onion is translucent. Add the nonreserved spiced chickpeas, watercress, salt, and boiling filtered water and simmer until the leaves wilt, about 3 minutes.

+ Transfer the mixture to a Vitamix and blend until smooth.

+ Taste and add salt to your liking.

+ Serve with the hot spiced carrots and reserved chickpeas.

3 carrots, diced into ¾-inch pieces

2 cups cooked chickpeas

2 tablespoons ras el hanout

2 tablespoons extra-virgin olive oil

1 onion, chopped

1 (1-inch) knob fresh ginger, grated

1 ½ to 2 bunches watercress

Himalayan pink salt

3 cups boiling filtered water

MI-SO HEALTHY

During my trip to Japan, I became enamored with the variety of their earthy and healthy miso-based broths. Miso, the prepared soy bean paste, is the most essential Japanese ingredient with a distinct umami flavor. Miso soups are a perfect start to every meal, including breakfast. Just one cup makes me feel loved, comforted, and grounded. Miso paste is easily found at natural food stores and Asian groceries (make sure you select organic paste with no MSG). This broth helps dissolve fat deposits and excess mucus throughout the body.

Serves 4

1 ½ cups daikon, sliced into ½-inch circles

1 quart spring water

1 (3-inch) piece wakame

3 teaspoons organic red miso paste

2 green onions, chopped, for serving

+ Place the daikon and spring water in a soup pot over medium heat and cook for 5 minutes.

+ Meanwhile, soak the wakame in water for 5 minutes and chop into small pieces.

+ Add the wakame to the pot and cook over low heat until the daikon and wakame are tender.

+ Dilute the miso paste in the stock, and simmer for another 3 minutes.

+ Serve immediately, topped with the green onions.

WHAT'S THE HURRY, MELON CURRY?

Bitter melons are considered lucky in Asia. Chinese doctors prescribe them as medicine for type 2 diabetes and there is actually science behind that. The compounds in melons appear to activate an enzyme that regulates metabolism and enables glucose uptake. Bitter melon is also an excellent source of B vitamins, iron, calcium, and beta-carotene. Combining yellow mung beans, fresh curry leaves, and potatoes, this East Asian–inspired soup is healing and cleansing, and could be just what the doctor ordered. You can find bitter melons at Asian markets and farmers markets.

Serves 4-6

1 tablespoon coconut oil

½ teaspoons fennel seeds

¼ teaspoon celery seeds

Pinch of fenugreek seeds

1 (1-inch) knob ginger, minced

1 medium-size red onion, chopped

½ teaspoon ground turmeric

2 bitter melons, sliced into circles (seeds and spongy insides discarded)

2 medium-size tomatoes, diced

10 curry leaves

1 bay leaf

1 tablespoon tamarind paste

Himalayan pink salt

1 cup dried yellow mung beans, washed

4 cups boiling filtered water

+ Drop the fennel seeds, celery seeds, and fenugreek seeds into a dry skillet and dry roast for a couple of minutes until the seeds flutter, releasing their essential oils and aromas.

+ Heat the oil in a soup pot over medium heat, add the ginger and onion, then the turmeric with dry-roasted spices, and sauté until the onion is tender and covered in spices.

+ Add the bitter melons, tomatoes, curry leaves, bay leaf, tamarind paste, and salt and mix together.

+ Add the mung beans and filtered water and cook over medium heat for 25 to 30 minutes, until the mung beans split open.

+ Taste and adjust the spices; the consistency should be thick and not too runny.

+ Discard the curry and bay leaves when serving.

Soupelina

BROTHS

Veggie Healing Broth, a.k.a. Lady MacBroth

Pho Sho

Lemongrass Cleansing Broth

Coconut Galangal Broth

Magic Turmeric Broth

Don't Kvass Me Any More Questions

Rejuvelak

Shake Your Tamarind

Soupelina

Pho Sho, page 180

VEGGIE HEALING BROTH,
A.K.A. LADY MACBROTH

I fell in love with this broth after just one spoonful. Every single ingredient is a superhero, and together, they turn into a magic potion: light, feisty, and satisfying, full of cancer- and disease-fighting properties. I love drinking it from a teacup with an extra sprinkle of cayenne or serve it loaded with fermented chopped veggies and fresh herbs, such as parsley, cilantro, or basil.

Serves 8

Boiling water, enough to cover mushrooms	2 carrots, peeled and chopped
5 whole dried shiitake mushrooms, washed	2 bok choy, halved
About 2 quarts spring water	1 (3-inch) piece daikon
½ bunch kale	3 garlic cloves, pounded
½ bunch collards	1 small knob (1 to 1 ½ inches) fresh ginger
½ bunch Swiss chard	½ Asian pear, halved (not peeled)
½ bunch mustard greens	A handful of cilantro
½ small cabbage, coarsely chopped	3 sprigs of thyme
½ fennel bulb, halved	A handful of parsley
½ medium-size onion, halved with skin	Himalayan pink salt

+ Pour boiling water over the washed dried shiitake mushrooms and leave them to soak for at least 30 minutes. Strain the mushrooms through a fine-mesh strainer into a clean container. Reserve the soaking water.

+ Combine the mushroom water with the spring water in a large pot and bring to a soft boil on medium heat.

+ Add all the ingredients except cilantro, thyme, parsley, and salt to the pot. If the veggies are too bulky, boil some more water and add to the pot so all the veggies are covered. Simmer for 2 hours.

+ Turn off the heat. Add the cilantro, thyme, and parsley. Steep for 15 minutes. Strain into another large pot, pressing on the solids in the strainer. Season with salt to taste. Let cool for at least 1 hour to allow the flavors to mature.

PHO SHO

I discovered pho during my trip to Vietnam. The interplay of textures and flavors in this aromatic traditional Vietnamese soup made me a pho fan, so naturally when I was back in LA, I began frequenting pho eateries all over the city: some were too salty, some were too sweet, and many were made with meat. I knew I had to re-create that special flavor I found in Hanoi. This broth is not just exotic tasting, it's an antiviral, immune-boosting, and cholesterol-lowering potion. Not to mention, if I'm on the verge of a cold or in need of a pick-me-up, this pho makes me feel better almost immediately. Adding the hing spice makes the soup extra special. Hing is one of the best digestion aids out there, it regulates blood sugar levels, relieves chest congestion, and protects against cancer. To see a photo of this soup, go to page 177.

Serves 8

Boiling water, enough to cover mushrooms

10 whole dried shiitake mushrooms, washed

1 medium-size yellow onion, peeled and halved

1 large knob fresh ginger, smashed

½ garlic bulb

4 carrots, scrubbed and roughly chopped

6 whole cloves

2 quarts spring water

1 whole Asian pear or apple, halved (not peeled)

1 (2-inch) piece daikon

1 leek, white and green part, roughly chopped

5 star anise

1 cinnamon stick

1 teaspoon coriander seeds

¼ cup tamari

1 teaspoon hing powder

Toppings

1 handful Thai fresh basil leaves

½ cup bean sprouts

1 Thai (bird's eye) chile, sliced

Lime

+ Pour boiling water over the washed and dried shiitake mushrooms and leave them to soak for at least 30 minutes. Strain the mushrooms through a fine-mesh strainer into a clean container. Reserve the soaking water.

+ Preheat a broiler, line a small baking sheet with foil, put the onion, ginger, garlic, and carrots on the prepared baking sheet, and broil for 5 minutes, until charred. Remove from the broiler, let cool enough to handle, then peel off the burned spots.

+ Stick the cloves into the peeled onion.

+ Combine the mushroom water with the spring water in a soup pot and bring to a boil.

+ Load with the broiled ingredients, Asian pear, daikon, and leek greens.

+ Simmer for 2 hours over medium-low heat.

+ While the broth is simmering, dry fry the star anise, cinnamon stick, and coriander seeds over medium heat.

+ Add the anise, coriander, and cinnamon to the broth, along with the hing and tamari, and simmer for another 30 minutes.

+ Pour the broth through a strainer. Discard all the solids, except the mushrooms.

+ Slice the mushrooms into thin strips.

+ Serve the broth with the sliced mushrooms, fresh basil, bean sprouts, Thai chile, and a squeeze of lime.

LEMONGRASS CLEANSING BROTH

This broth is surprising and a totally new way to enjoy the cleansing benefits of lemongrass. If you've never cooked with lemongrass before, you will love the slightly lemony but complex and refreshing flavors of it, especially when combined with galangal, kaffir lime leaves, and shiitake mushrooms. The flavor burst is insane! And so are the health benefits: The broth is alkalizing, cleansing, refreshing, and anti-inflammatory.

Serves 8

2 whole dried shiitake
mushrooms, washed

2 quarts spring water

4 cups coarsely chopped
cabbage

1 large onion, peeled and
quartered

6 fresh shiitake mushrooms

1 fennel bulb, halved

5 large lemongrass stalks, cut
into 4-inch pieces, halved
and pounded

1 large garlic bulb, cut in half
crosswise

1 bunch fresh cilantro with roots

1 large knob fresh ginger,
smashed

4 kaffir lime leaves, torn

1 to 2 Thai (bird's eye) chiles

½ cup chopped fresh Thai basil

½ cup chopped fresh mint

Himalayan pink salt

+ Pour boiling water over the washed dried shiitake mushrooms and leave them to soak for at least 30 minutes. Strain the mushrooms through a fine-mesh strainer into a clean container. Reserve the soaking water.

+ Combine the mushroom water with the spring water in a large pot and bring to a boil.

+ Add all the ingredients except the Thai basil, mint, and salt, to the pot. Simmer for 2 hours.

+ Turn off the heat. Add the Thai basil and mint. Steep 15 minutes. Strain into another large pot, pressing on the solids in the strainer.

+ Season with salt to taste.

+ Let cool for 1 hour to absorb the flavors.

NOTE
Try shredded green papaya (another Thai staple) and Thai basil leaves when serving. Together, they add crunch and extra health benefits.

Soupelina

COCONUT GALANGAL BROTH

This creamy broth packs a punch, and the first time I made it, I did a happy dance in my kitchen. It also felt like a happy dance in my mouth. The broth is admittedly special and high-lights Thai flavors, without them overwhelming one another. The delicate aroma and flavor that comes from galangal in contrast to coconut milk and lime juice create an addictive but healthy concoction.

Serves 8

2 cups light coconut milk

7 slices young galangal

3 stalks lemongrass, cut into 1-inch-long pieces and bruised

1 medium-size sweet potato, peeled and sliced into 1-inch rounds

4 kaffir lime leaves, torn

5 cups spring water

1 tablespoon Himalayan pink salt

2 ½ teaspoons freshly squeezed lime juice

Fresh cilantro sprigs, for garnish

+ Heat the coconut milk in a soup pot over medium heat and bring to a boil.

+ When boiling, add the galangal, lemongrass, sweet pota-to, and kaffir lime leaves.

+ Lower the heat, add the spring water, cover, and simmer for an hour.

+ Remove from the heat and let stand for about 20 min-utes to absorb the flavors.

+ Discard the veggies and season with the salt and lime juice.

+ Garnish with fresh cilantro sprigs and serve hot.

Soupelina

NOTE

If you'd like the broth creamy, add 1 ½ cups of coconut milk before adding the spring water to the pot.

MAGIC TURMERIC BROTH

Turmeric is a wonder spice! In Ayurveda, it is honored as a symbol of prosperity and pre-scribed to cleanse the entire body. Its amazing digestive properties heal your gut, and it helps with fevers, infections, and arthritis, not to mention being one of the best preventative reme-dies. In my broth, I marry it with coconut oil, another natural wonder; garlic, a known cancer fighter; and the cleansing ginger. The result is nothing short of magic.

Serves 8

+ Preheat the oven to 375°F.

+ Arrange the carrots on a baking sheet and toss with half of the thyme, a drizzle of olive oil, and salt. Roast for about 20 minutes, until browned in spots and soft.

+ Meanwhile, heat the coconut oil in a soup pot over medium-low heat, add the shallot, and sauté until trans-lucent and soft, around 3 minutes.

+ Add the garlic, ginger, and the rest of thyme. Stir until the mix is fragrant, then add the turmeric.

+ Continue stirring until the mixture becomes pasty, about 3 minutes. Add more coconut oil if it becomes too dry.

+ Add the roasted carrots and saffron to the mixture, then the spring water, and gently simmer the broth for about 2 hours.

+ Turn off the heat. Leave on the stove for another hour to absorb the flavors.

+ Add the lemon juice and season with salt and pepper to taste.

+ Strain the broth.

+ Garnish with fresh thyme, sprouts, or sesame seeds.

4 medium-size carrots, scrubbed and sliced lengthwise

4 fresh thyme sprigs

Extra-virgin olive oil, for roasting

Himalayan pink salt

2 tablespoons coconut oil

1 shallot, chopped

3 garlic cloves

1 thumb-size piece fresh ginger, peeled and minced

2 teaspoons ground turmeric

4 threads saffron

8 cups spring water

Juice of 1/2 lemon

Freshly ground black pepper

Fresh thyme, sprouts, or sesame seeds, for garnish

DON'T KVASS ME ANYMORE QUESTIONS

This recipe comes straight from my family's kitchen. Beet kvass has a long Russian history and I bet you will have a hard time finding a Russian who won't tell you all the health benefits of kvass. My grandma drank it to help her with her high blood pressure and heart issues and swore by its benefits. Fermented beets are sort of a magic bullet when it comes to health; they are packed with antioxidants, they have plenty of carotenes and nitrates, and most important, beets contain a precursor to glutathione, the prime detox agent in the liver that rids the body of toxins. Beet kvass is super easy to make. I almost always have it on hand for a quick probiotic effect.

Serves 4

4 small organic beets, cleaned, trimmed, scrubbed, and cubed

3 garlic cloves

2 tablespoons Himalayan pink salt

¼ teaspoon mustard seeds

¼ teaspoon dill seeds

Spring or filtered water

A few fresh dill sprigs (optional)

+ Place the beets in a clean quart-size jar.

+ Add the garlic, salt, mustard seeds, and dill seeds.

+ Fill the jar with spring or filtered water, leaving a 1-inch space at the top of the jar.

+ Place the fresh dill sprigs on top.

+ Cover the jar and let it ferment at room temperature for 2 to 3 days. Open the jar daily to taste the liquid and skim off any foam from the top.

+ When it tastes strong for you, strain and refrigerate. You can use the liquid for your cold borscht and pickled beets in salads or as a snack.

Soupelina

REJUVELAK

Rich in B vitamins and vitamins E and K, this fermented drink is a probiotic and amazing for your gut flora. Drink it between your meals for energy and improved digestion.

1 cup dried organic quinoa (it helps to buy special quinoa for sprouting)

3 cups filtered or purified water, plus more for fermenting

+ Place the quinoa in a 1-gallon glass jar and add an inch of water on top. Cover with cheesecloth and let stand overnight.

+ Drain the water, then rinse the quinoa water two or three times with room-temperature water. Drain all the water again.

+ Set the jar away from light and let it sit for 6 to 8 hours. When you see little tail sprouts on the quinoa kernels, you will know it's ready.

+ Add filtered or purified water to the sprouts to fill the jar, and let it ferment at room temperature for 2 more days.

+ The Rejuvelak should taste tart and sour, and have a yellow tint. It should not taste like sour milk.

+ Strain and refrigerate for up to 1 week.

SHAKE YOUR TAMARIND

Let's talk tamarind. Have you tried this tangy, beanlike pod fruit, popular in South India, Indonesia, and Thailand? Known for centuries for its comforting and healing properties, tamarind is made into soups and drinks, and added to food. This recipe is inspired by South Indian rasam broth, a hot and sour soup infused with exotic herbs and spices, praised for its Ayurvedic properties and excellent for cold, coughs, and sore throats. In India, this soup is considered a cure for all that ails. It's grounding and provides an intense awakening for your senses. In India, rasam soup is served at the end of the meal as a digestif.

Serves 4-6

+ Grind the peppercorns, cumin seeds, and curry leaves and mash together in a mortar and pestle.

+ Puree the tomatoes with a little water.

+ Bring the spring water to a boil in a soup pot, add the tamarind paste, and lower the heat to a simmer.

+ Add the tomatoes, salt, ground spices, and turmeric to the tamarind water and simmer together for about 10 minutes.

+ In a separate saucepan, heat the oil, drop in the mustard seeds, and toast until they crackle. Add the fenugreek seeds and chiles and cook until the aroma fills your kitchen, about 2 minutes.

+ Pour the chile mixture into the soup and season to taste.

+ Garnish with fresh cilantro leaves.

1 teaspoon black peppercorns

1 tablespoon cumin seeds

10 curry leaves

2 plum tomatoes, quartered

4 cups spring water, plus more to puree the tomatoes

2 teaspoons tamarind paste

Himalayan pink salt

¼ teaspoon ground turmeric

1 tablespoon coconut oil

¼ teaspoon mustard seeds

¼ teaspoon fenugreek seeds

2 medium-size dried red chile peppers

Fresh cilantro leaves, for garnish

NOTE

You can buy tamarind paste at natural food stores or Asian markets.

RAW SOUPS

What the Hemp?

I'm Pumpkin Myself Up

Thai Me Up, Thai Me Down Gazpacho

Brave New Watermelon

A-Lotta Avocado

Macho Gazpacho

Mint, Take a Hint!

WHAT THE HEMP?

This recipe is inspired by my mom's cold Russian soup recipe. In Russia, it is made with kefir and meat, but it is fresher and way more nutritious raw and vegan. Hemp milk, apple cider vinegar, and lemon juice help break down fats and reduce glucose levels, and the pectin in apple cider vinegar helps remove toxic metals and residues of radiation. Hemp's omega-3 fatty acids support healthy brain function, and the milk also contains antioxidant vitamin E, which contributes to the glowing skin. This soup will energize you and offer you great immune protection. To see a photo of this soup, go to pages 88-89.

Serves 4

4 cups hemp milk

2 tablespoons raw organic unpasteurized apple cider vinegar

1 teaspoon Himalayan pink salt

2 medium-size avocados, cubed

3 Persian cucumbers, sliced into semicircles

5 radishes, sliced into semicircles

½ cup fresh dill, minced

½ bunch green onions, sliced

2 tablespoons freshly squeezed lemon juice

Freshly ground black pepper (optional)

+ Mix the hemp milk, apple cider vinegar, and salt in a large bowl.

+ Add half of the avocado cubes. Transfer the mixture to a Vitamix and blend.

+ Pour the mixture back into the bowl and add all the sliced veggies, including the remaining avocado, along with the dill and lemon juice.

+ Taste and adjust the salt, lemon juice, and apple cider vinegar; add pepper if needed.

+ Chill in the fridge and serve cold.

I'M PUMPKIN MYSELF UP

I love discovering different ways to cook with pumpkins. I used to think they were for Halloween decoration only, but the more I experiment, the more gaga I get over them. This soup is extremely easy to prepare and it's such a potent B vitamins and beta-carotene potion. In Chinese nutrition, pumpkin is considered a cancer-prevention food. But it also relieves eczema, regulates blood sugar balance, and benefits the pancreas. Pairing the pumpkin with garlic and ginger helps eliminate toxins from the body. To see a photo of this soup, go to pages 88-89.

Serves 4

+ Combine all the ingredients, except your desired garnish, in a Vitamix and puree until it's very smooth and fluffy.

+ Taste and adjust the salt and spices. If the soup is too thick, add some more water until it reaches your desired consistency.

+ Garnish with dill, pepitas, or sunflower seeds.

½ medium-size organic pumpkin, peeled, seeded, and cut into cubes

½ cup organic pepitas

2 tablespoons fresh dill, minced

1 ½ teaspoons Himalayan pink salt

1 garlic clove

1 (1-inch) piece fresh ginger

1 teaspoon yellow curry powder

2 cups spring water

Fresh dill, pepitas, or sunflower seeds, for garnish

NOTE

You can warm the soup to 110°F to preserve its enzymes. When pumpkins are out of season, make this soup with butternut squash; it's just as delicious! I also like to replace the curry powder with turmeric, when I feel that I want a milder flavor.

THAI ME UP, THAI ME DOWN GAZPACHO

Here is another Thai soup recipe. I told you, Thai food is an obsession for me. But it's so much more than that. Thai cuisine is super healthy and every bite tastes like a trip; don't you agree? Cold soups are a once-in-a-while thing for me, as I love the warmth and comfort of hot soups. So, if I do eat cold, it has to be a flavor bomb. This soup is not a traditional Thai recipe; it's my fusion take on Thai. To see a photo of this soup, go to pages 88-89.

Serves 4

+ Combine the cucumbers, green onions, garlic, half of the Thai chile, and the water in a food processor or Vitamix.

+ Process until a puree is formed. With the blender running, slowly add the remaining ingredients. Mix until combined.

+ Taste and adjust the salt and spices.

+ Chill until ready to serve.

3 cucumbers, peeled and chopped

4 green onions, sliced

2 garlic cloves, pressed and minced

1 Thai (a.k.a. bird's eye) chile, sliced

1 cup chilled spring water

3 cilantro sprigs

1 tablespoon reduced-sodium tamari

2 tablespoons rice vinegar

1 teaspoon sesame oil

Juice of 1 lime

BRAVE NEW WATERMELON

After making this soup, you will never throw watermelon rinds away again. I actually save mine every time I eat a watermelon! Who knew that the pale pink and green part contain an amino acid called citrulline that plays a key role in our urea cycle, which removes nitrogen from our blood and converts it to urine? It's such a powerful antioxidant that scientists are actually considering producing a supplement from watermelon rind, because it also helps with cardiovascular issues. But while they are busy conceiving the supplement, you can enjoy this refreshing and oh so yummy watermelon gazpacho.

Serves 4-6

+ Combine the mint, celery, garlic, tomatoes, and oil in a Vitamix. Puree until smooth. Transfer the mixture to a large bowl.

+ Working in batches if necessary, combine the cucumbers, watermelon rind, apple cider vinegar, and salt in the Vitamix. Puree until as chunky or smooth as desired.

+ Add to the other puree and stir together well. Taste, adding salt and vinegar as needed.

+ Chill until cold, about 2 hours. Taste for salt again before serving.

1 cup loosely packed fresh mint leaves, or mint and parsley leaves

1 celery stalk, cut into chunks

1 garlic clove

1 dozen cherry tomatoes

2 tablespoons extra-virgin olive oil

4 Persian cucumbers, cut into chunks

4 cups cubed organic watermelon rind, pale pink and green parts, hard skin removed

1 tablespoon apple cider vinegar

1 tablespoon Himalayan pink salt

A-LOTTA AVOCADO

Oh, avocados! Their velvety-smooth texture is so delicious and their health benefits so great, you just can't have too many of these magical green superfruits. This soup will fuel you, refresh you, and shower your body with alkalizing goodness. Breast cancer protection . . . check! Oral cancer defense . . . check! Eye health, heart health, better nutrient absorption, and an excellent source of glutathione and vitamin E: This soup has it all. Enjoy it for breakfast, lunch, or snack. To see a photo of this soup, go to pages 88-89.

Serves 4

2 medium-size avocados,
   peeled and seeded

4 organic Persian cucumbers,
   roughly chopped

Juice of 1 lime

2 garlic cloves

1 zucchini, roughly chopped

1 teaspoon Himalayan
   pink salt

¼ to ½ cup fresh cilantro

¾ cup spring water

Watermelon radish, thinly
   sliced, for garnish

+ Place all the ingredients, except the watermelon radish, in a Vitamix and puree until your desired consistency is reached.

+ Taste, and adjust the salt and lime juice.

+ Transfer to a glass bowl and chill in the fridge before serving.

+ Garnish with watermelon radish and serve.

MACHO GAZPACHO

I love a good gazpacho. It reminds me of the summers I spent in Italy and Spain, where a bowl of gazpacho is a typical start to a healthy meal. Besides watermelon gazpacho, this tomato version is a must on a hot summer day. For me, it's a salad in liquid form: it takes minutes to prepare and you get all the health benefits from this antioxidant-rich soup, including reduced stress. I like my gazpacho chunky and with a little kick, just like the one I had in Barcelona. To see a photo of this soup, go to pages 88-89.

Serves 4-6

+ Combine the tomato juice, chopped tomatoes and their juice, cucumbers, garlic, celery, onion, bell pepper, jalapeño, and apple cider vinegar in a Vitamix and blend until your desired consistency is reached. Alternatively, you can use a handheld blender.

+ Add the olive oil, season with salt and pepper, and refrigerate.

+ Serve with radish sprouts.

1 cup freshly pressed tomato juice

6 ripe tomatoes, chopped, with juice

2 Persian cucumbers, chopped

2 garlic cloves, minced

1 celery stalk

½ red onion, chopped

1 red bell pepper, chopped

½ to 1 jalapeño pepper

2 tablespoon apple cider vinegar

1 ½ teaspoons extra-virgin olive oil

Himalayan pink salt and freshly ground black pepper

Radish sprouts, for garnish

MINT, TAKE A HINT!

This soup almost doesn't feel like soup. I eat it as a snack or a pick-me-up. But don't let the lightness fool you into thinking that this is not a supersoup! Cucumbers are a great source of B vitamins, rehydrate your body, and help eliminate toxins. And did you know that cucumbers have most of the vitamins our body needs in a single day? I like Persian cucumbers because of their sweet skin; I would never peel them because their skins are packed with vitamin C. One of my favorite cucumber soup-er powers is its cocktail of lignans (lariciresinol, pinoresinol, and secoisolariciresinol) that are known to fight cancer, including breast, ovarian, uterine, and prostate. Paired with mint, it's a great breath refresher and stimulates hair growth. The sesame seeds provide protein, and leek brings the bite. Yum!

Serves 4-6

5 Persian cucumbers
  (3 juiced, 2 chopped)

¼ leek, chopped

2 tablespoons sesame seeds,
  soaked

2 tablespoons sunflower
  seeds, soaked

¼ cup fresh mint, plus more
  for garnish

Himalayan pink salt

+ Place the juiced and chopped cucumbers in a Vitamix, add the leek, soaked seeds, mint, and salt to taste.

+ Blend until liquid smooth.

+ Chill before serving, then garnish with fresh mint.

HOW TO SOAK SEEDS

Soaking seeds for your soup recipes is an important step. Not only does soaking activate nutrients (especially Viataims A, B, and C) but it also neutralizes enzyme inhibitors, promotes the growth of digestive enzymes, and makes seeds easier to digest.

1 cup raw, untoasted seeds

2 cups filtered or spring water (2:1 ratio)

+ Place the seeds in a glass bowl or mason jar, cover with room temperature water, and soak overnight.

+ Drain and throw away the soak water.

+ Rinse the seeds.

+ Paper-towel dry the seeds.

Soupelina

8

I AM DONE WITH THE CLEANSE; NOW WHAT?

You did it! Hip, hip, hooray! How are you feeling, my super-soupie?

I know you are proud of yourself. You feel clear, happy, and energetic. You've most likely dropped a few pounds, your skin is glowing, your hair is shiny, and your mood has improved. You began to listen to your body and understand its signals. But most important, you have started to create an environment that will fight off any viruses or bacteria and keep you healthy.

I know you don't want to return to your previous lifestyle and eating habits. "But I can't live on soups forever," you say. Here is the thing: With the popularity of cleanses, I feel that anyone can do a cleanse, but it's what happens *after* the cleanse that matters. The soup cleanse you've just completed is designed to kick-start a new lifestyle for you, the more balanced lifestyle that includes healthy habits. This is a very special opportunity; take advantage of it! Don't blow it!

I'm not just saying this—I know it! When I started feeling better after my first cleanse, I thought I could have a few bites of the foods I'd stopped eating, foods I knew weren't good for me; but hey, isn't everything good in moderation? Well, I don't believe in that anymore. You know already how much I love bread, so I thought having a slice or two with a great salad after my cleanse would be fine. Seriously, what was I thinking? I woke up the next morning feeling sluggish and craving coffee. The entire day, I felt off, my energy level was low, and all I could think of was having more bread.

If you want to hang on to what you've already achieved, take some time to map out your post-cleanse transitioning. Remember, there is no "one-size-fits-all" approach. This is your journey and you know what's best for you! Sometimes, you just need a little nudge.

Continuing the Cleanse

Go ahead, pat yourself on the back; you deserve it! This was a great start. But if you are serious about your cleanse, continue it for at least three weeks, and stretch to three or even four months if you are trying to clear a health condition. It doesn't mean you have to live on soups for that long, but soups and broths will become a staple in your daily diet. Incorporate fresh salads and pack them with veggies, fresh and fermented, along with legumes, sprouts, and whole grains, such as quinoa, black, brown and red rice, buckwheat, and farro. Eat fruits and berries for snacks, but not as dessert after a meal.

It takes around four months for the body to replace all the red blood cells. White blood cells renew more often: from a few hours to a few days and about ten days for platelets. All this means is that if you follow this plan (cleanse, followed by clean, plant-based diet with daily soups) for at least four months, all the new blood cells will be created healthy.

If you decide to continue, make sure you vary the menu to avoid too much weight loss. If that happens, add more oil into your diet; you can double the oil in the recipes.

Breaking the Cleanse

To keep your post-cleanse glow, start the transition slowly. Kudos if you decide to continue eating plant-based meals at the end of your cleanse, but if you are a devoted meat eater, give it some time. For every food you reintroduce, ask yourself the following questions, to check in with your body. Write the answers in your journal, it's super helpful to look back at the answers even a week later; you immediately see patterns.

+ How do I feel after eating it?

+ What happens immediately: Do I get a runny nose or mucus in my throat (happens without fail if I touch a piece of cheese or any other dairy)?

+ Do I feel tired after my meal or the next morning (happens to me every time I have a glass of wine or indulge in baked goods)?

+ How's my poop?

+ Did I sleep well?

+ Is my energy high?

+ How's my skin? Do I have a pimple? Any redness, dry patches, dullness?

+ Are my nails strong? Is my hair luscious?

+ Am I cranky the next day? Do I feel bad about things?

+ Do I have a headache?

When I asked myself these questions, I learned that everything depends on what I eat and how I take care of my body. I've become so good at diagnosing myself that I know when things are off almost immediately. And I still can't believe that we have so much control over how we feel on a daily basis. When you really pay attention to what you eat and how the food makes you feel, you really can help yourself to heal.

I know you are a smart soup-er, but I still have to warn you:

+ Avoid fast foods, packaged foods, and fried foods, especially after enjoying days of delectable veggies, herbs, and legumes.

+ Stay away from animal protein for a least a week and then slowly bring it back once or twice a week; otherwise it will undo all your cleansing efforts, not to mention make you feel gassy and bloated. And that's so not sexy.

+ Don't slip. By this point your cravings have most likely gone away and it will not be hard for you. But if you are not used to eating whole foods, you may experience a desire to binge on certain foods. If you think you might slip, create an action plan. That way when the urge appears, you will be ready.

+ Don't fool yourself that any form of dairy is okay: Not only will your skin break out, but you will most likely feel tired and lack energy. You have just learned that your body doesn't need as much as you thought it did and it feels better when you nourish it with good organic soups.

+ Continue with soups for breakfast and dinner, and pay attention to your body when you reintroduce other foods.

+ Introduce fruits (best to start with berries, apples, pears, prunes, peaches, and tangerines), but continue to stay away from any other form of sugar, even agave, maple syrup, and stevia. Also, no sodas, no alcohol, no coffee, no candy or sweets, no bread, and no dairy! Make your own "do not eat" list and check in with it. Be careful with snacking. Munch on raw and fermented veggies, radishes, roasted seaweed, kale chips, and seeds.

+ Eat plenty of probiotic-rich foods, such as sauerkraut, kimchi, and pickles, and drink probiotic-rich drinks, such as kombucha, coconut kefir, kvass, and Rejuvelak. This is very important after a cleanse; you want to replenish your intestinal flora with friendly bacteria and improve your digestion. We will chat more about that later when I speak with Dr. Gerard Mullin, the leading authority on gut health.

Soup Cleanse Seasonally

Seasonal Soup Cleanse is a great way to transition into a new time of year and enjoy the goodness of each season. Ancient medicines believe that our body functions best when we stay in tune with nature and follow the seasons; Ayurveda and Traditional Chinese Medicine teach that routine cleansing is invaluable for maintaining good health during seasonal changes. It empowers us to get in harmony with ourselves, our environment, and the cycles of nature.

Have you noticed that you get more colds in the fall or winter and feel more tired or sluggish in the spring? Have you ever thought about the term *under the weather* and where it came from? What you do need is to stay in balance and maintain your well-being by taking care of your body—especially when seasons change, because our body mirrors those changes. This allows your cells, tissues, organs, and bodily fluids to flush any toxins before they add up to dangerous levels and you are at risk of getting sick.

At the end of the day, cleansing simply means giving your body a rest. And making meals for yourself is a profound way to show self-love. Cleansing seasonally is not just eating Soupelina's nutritious soups, it's also aligning the mind-set, the emotions, and the spirit with each season. If that's too ambitious and you only want to do it once, cleanse in the spring. For those who ask, "What if I cleanse twice a year?" I say do it in the spring and fall.

Keep the Toxins Out of Your Kitchen and Your Body

Your body needs nutrients, plain and simple. Eating produce that has been treated with chemicals, pesticides, growth hormones, GMOs, and other harmful sprays is just not okay in my book. And while most states are fighting the GMO bills, why worry whether your veggies are contributing to your cell mutations? Besides, organic food just tastes better.

Studies from the 1990s show that organic produce averaged twice the mineral content of the supermarket nonorganic food! And a 2014 study done in the UK found that organic foods contain higher levels of antioxidants, and lower levels of toxic metals and pesticides.

There are times when you just don't have a choice. In those cases, make sure that you are at least not eating veggies from the "dirty dozen" list, and soak/peel/scrub your veggies well. Perhaps you've seen the list compiled by the Environmental Working Group, but if you haven't, here it is again, along with the "clean fifteen." I know you are a smarty-pants soup cleanser, but I just have to warn you.

The DIRTY dozen

1. Peach	7. Cherries
2. Apple	8. Kale
3. Bell pepper	9. Lettuce
4. Celery	10. Grapes
5. Nectarine	11. Carrot
6. Strawberries	12. Pear

The CLEAN fifteen

1. Onion	9. Cabbage
2. Avocado	10. Eggplant
3. Sweet corn	11. Papaya
4. Pineapple	12. Watermelon
5. Mango	13. Broccoli
6. Asparagus	14. Tomato
7. Sweet peas	15. Sweet potato
8. Kiwi	

Soupelina

Shopping for Your Food

I'm one lucky girl. I live in sunny California and we have farmers markets seven days a week. But I bet your town has at least one farmers market close by. Go there! It's the best single thing you can do to improve your relationship with food and with yourself.

You will see what's in season and buy the freshest produce from the farms just hours from where you live. You will discover new things and get to sample them before buying. You are also more likely to buy from the person who grows the food. I think there is something magical about that, making your relationship with the soup you cook stronger. And more affordable. The farmers will help you select the firmest greens, the most fragrant tomatoes, and the best-looking squash. You can also ask questions about how the produce was grown, what's really tasty, and the best ways to use fruits and veggies that may be new to you.

I love shopping at the Santa Monica and Studio City farmers markets, near where I live. You can find me there three times a week (please say hello when you see me!) and I don't ever have a list. My favorite farmers know my taste and sometimes hold things for me, I chat with them and people who are shopping that day, at times explaining why I buy a certain vegetable or herb and what I do with it. Occasionally, my chats turn into recipe sharing and phone number exchanging. Like the sweet lady I met last week when I was buying lemons, offering to give me all the lemons from her lemon tree when I told her I use some in my soups. (See, soup really does bring people together!) Having the connection to the people who grow my ingredients helps me appreciate what I make out of them and eat even more.

Depending on where you live, other shopping options are Whole Foods, Sprouts, local co-ops, other natural food stores, and small ethnic stores: Asian, Russian, Indian, Middle Eastern, and Latin American, or larger international markets that stock products from all over the world, such as the ones I was used to in the Atlanta area when I lived there. Just do a little research; you'd be amazed at the gems you will find. Wherever you shop, buy preferably local and organic.

Eating on the Go

Soup is the ultimate convenience food: It's filling, it's good for you, and you can carry it around! But what happens if you are out of town or have to stay at work late? Prepare your soups in advance and always have them around, especially if you are on a cleanse. Have a few containers in the freezer for emergencies; you just never know. If you decide to commit to the soup lifestyle and take it with you when you are out of town, consider investing in a small blender, such as NutriBullet, which you can travel with. Pick your favorite raw recipes and make raw soups anywhere. It's really easy, all it takes is a little prep. Another trick is to travel with the miso paste and dried wakame; you can make a hot miso soup anywhere, even on an airplane. All you have to ask for is hot water.

Soupelina

9

LISTEN TO YOUR GUT

What Is Your Gut Telling You?

We all love to talk about our "gut instincts" and "gut feelings," but how much do you know about your gut? Why do we want to know what takes place in our intestines? Should we be worried?

Okay, ladies and gentlemen, listen up. It's *all* about our gut! Now that you know a lot about your body, let's examine its most underappreciated organ—your gut. Did you know that our gut is what makes us who we are?

After centuries of ignoring the most famous doctor (yes, I'm talking about Hippocrates), who proclaimed that "all disease begins in the gut," we are finally realizing that it turns out our gut is pretty miraculous: It helps us digest our foods, it helps educate our immune system, it helps us resist disease, and it may even be responsible for our behavior. In other words, there is a lot going on down there.

In fact, it's now the new frontier in medicine: the study of our microbiome. I mentioned the term *second brain* in Chapter 2; that's what our digestive system is being called nowadays. It's actually an official name accepted by medical professionals and it was Dr. Michael Gershon, a professor at Columbia University, who coined it. After thirty years of studying the gut, Dr.

Gershon confirmed that our digestive system has its own cerebral activity and intelligence. Yup, two brains are better than one.

Now you understand that there's no way we can control our digestive functions with our mind. Our powerful mental control stops the moment we start eating. So, start paying attention to your gut and amazing things will happen. Whether you picked up this book to lose weight or heal from a chronic condition, your gut will most likely hold the answers you've been looking for. Because it's not enough to just eat right; it's absorbing the goodness of the organic ingredients that's so important.

Let's get a few things out of the way. If you are a health nut like me, you know that our body is made up of over 100 trillion microbes and they live (and die) on every single part of our body. The largest concentrations of them are in our tummy and it's called gut flora, or microbiome. (Such a fancy name!) For every one human cell in your body, there are nine cells of bacteria: Think of them as good bacteria and bad bacteria.

I asked my daughter Isabelle to illustrate the way she saw the good vs. the bad guys in her tummy. She is the artist behind the Soupelina fairy, and here is her good vs. bad bacteria drawing.

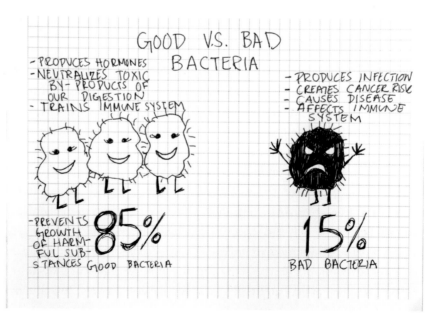

Gut Balance

*with Dr. Gerard Mullin, MD, gastrointerologist, nutritionist,
gut microbiome authority*

To really understand what it's all about, I turned to Dr. Gerard Mullin, the leading authority on gut health. As Associate Professor of Medicine at the Johns Hopkins University School of Medicine and author of *The Gut Balance Revolution*, Dr. Mullin has been advocating gut health for decades. Who better than him to explain what's what?

EF: How do you know that your gut is out of balance?

GM: You'll have gas, bloating, altered [excessive or lack of] bowel movements, but sometimes your symptoms can be "silent," like headaches, you can have fatigue, you can have migraines, you can have joint aches. These are symptoms that are broadcast directly from the gut. For thousands of years, Ayurvedic medicine and Hippocrates, and Elie Mechnikov [Russian-born biologist and Nobel laureate who made the first direct link between human longevity and healthy gut bacteria] honored the gut: all these people that taught us about health and we've disregarded it only until the last five years. We've ignored how important that is. The world revolves around the gut.

EF: Why have we disregarded the importance of the gut?

GM: It was René Descartes, a seventeenth-century philosopher and scientist, who introduced the concept of reductionism in medicine, which began the unfortunate modern era of compartmentalizing the body into distinct independent systems; thus specialists were born. That led the medicine down the garden pathway to specialists and medications being the magic bullets.

We have been brainwashed and led down the road to destruction by these pharmaceutical companies and all the dirty politics through medical schools and legislature that really allowed them to prey on us. A lot of the diseases that we see, as much as they are being treated by pharmaceuticals, are being caused by pharmaceuticals. All this feeds into the people who profit off of us. As we become more dependent on pharmaceuticals, we are relying on magic bullets and that's how our society has been functioning. And it doesn't help us. It hurts us.

EF: We are hearing a lot about the gut these days.

GM: It's like the world is awakening; people now see the connection. Look at you: You had breast cancer and you had no idea that you had a problem with your gut. Your health depends on a healthy gut.

Today we are experiencing the modern-day renaissance when it comes to gut health. You see the books come out, you see myself, you see [David] Perlmutter's *Brain Maker*, and others. Now is the time! For many years, people were dismissed for being quacks, people like the naturopaths, the functional medicine doctors . . . now the data is validating and confirming what these people have been doing for decades. For me, it's gratifying! But the gut health has a long tradition: TCM [Traditional Chinese Medicine] and Ayurvedic medicine were all predicated upon the gut as the central controller of health and wellness. As Elie Mechnikov said, "Death begins in the colon."

EF: What do people need to know about rebalancing their gut?

GM: Restrict the foods that can injure your gut (antibiotics are the modern plague; they are disrupting the gut and causing superbugs, obesity, you name it). I would restrict those bad actors that are ruining our gut flora and our health. Then, rebalance from the stress of life because under stress, your acidity, your enzyme production, and your gut flora will all suffer and you will have a very messed up gut environment unless you learn to relax. Rejuvenation and restoring your flora is next; once you start raking the leaves and start taking those weeds out and rebuilding the soil with really good prebiotic foods, like asparagus, Jerusalem artichokes, onions, garlic, dandelion—these veggies all have the healthy bifidobacteria and help you really increase your biodiversity in the gut. Be regular about your bowel movements. And if you have a leaky gut, which a lot of people do, you are allowing all the toxins to recirculate and you are really hurting yourself . . . you have to be mindful of your bowel movements. And sleep. Restorative sleep is very important because besides depression and obesity, lack of sleep alters your microbiome. It's all about a healthy lifestyle and part of the healthy lifestyle is to have restorative sleep and not try to cheat your body out of sleep by doing caffeine and sugar.

Goupelina

EF: How can soups and broths help with healing the gut?

GM: There is a long tradition of healing the gut with soups and broths and actually boosting your immunity, as you knew going through your cancer. Your soups and broths were very much helping you fight your cancer.

Once people start to reboot and get rid of the junk and weed out some of the bad bugs and allow their inner ecosystems to thrive, their lives will change.

EF: How important is it to cleanse your gut?

GM: Good question. Some believe that there should be a seasonal "cleanse" to reboot the gut. I say, be gentle and shift the microbiome in phases. Here's how: (1) Reboot by cutting off the supply of pathogens that smother the growth of our friendly flora, by cutting out refined carbs, high-sugary foods, inflammatory fats, and GMO-rich foods, such as wheat, high fructose foods, etc. (2) Reseed and refeed the gut. It's like planting a garden: You weed, fertilize, then seed to establish a foundation. (3) Feed with fertilizing prebiotic foods, such as asparagus, artichoke, and veggies that lay the foundation for those fermented foods, which contain live cultures that help you thrive.

EF: How do you listen to your gut?

GM: It's very difficult to do in our fast-paced, crazy world. I think many of us who refer to "gut instinct" do so because somehow there is an unconscious awareness that an inner voice is guiding our thoughts and behaviors to influence decisions. Once a mystery, we now know from a variety of experiments, that the gut and its microbes can influence our thoughts and decision-making process. Listening to your gut in illness is not the same as in health. That's why prevention is so important, not just intervention when illness strikes. We all need to be less reactive and more proactive. The gut is the second brain and has a very strong bidirectional communication with our brain and vice versa. If you want to be smarter, razor sharp, harmonious, and resilient, don't take a pill; cultivate a happy and balanced gut!

DR. GERARD MULLIN'S PRESCRIPTION FOR GUT HEALTH

Restrict the foods that can injure your gut, such as caffeine, sugar, sodas, refined carbs, high-sugary foods, inflammatory fats, and GMO-rich foods, such as wheat, high-fructose foods, etc.

Avoid antibiotics whenever possible.

Fill your diet with prebiotic foods, such as asparagus, Jerusalem artichokes, onions, garlic, and dandelion.

Be regular about your bowel movements.

Get ample restorative sleep.

Younger Skin

with Harold Lancer, MD, Fellow of the American Academy of Dermatology

I know you are in a hurry to get your gut cleaned but that pimple on your chin is really driving you crazy.

I get it.

Is there a soup that can help clear your skin up, you think?

I'm here to help.

Actually, I decided to invite dermatologist Dr. Harold Lancer, Hollywood's foremost authority on radiant skin, to help. He is the man behind many beautiful faces you see on the big and small screens. But what I love most about Dr. Lancer is that he is constantly testing plants, herbs, and anything that can make our skin gorgeous. And guess what is his breakthrough antiaging method for radiant skin?

EF: So, feeding your skin is the most important thing you can do?

HL: What you put in your body is what you will get out of it. Your energy levels, your mood, your skin, and your day-to-day well-being are all influenced by what you eat and drink. The better you are about supplying your

Soupelina

body with the nutrients and fuel it needs and avoiding the empty calories of junk food, the better you will look and feel.

EF: I love that you ask your patients about their diet because, let's face it, how we look is an indicator of our overall health. What is your favorite advice to your patients who want blemish-free skin?

HL: I first tell new patients to drop any and all processed, prepackaged food from their diets. It's astonishing just how many people don't understand that frozen meals, protein bars, etc. contain little to no nutrients and extremely high levels of sodium and sugar, which wreak havoc on the skin.

I then encourage my patients to incorporate fresh greens into their diets, eaten raw when possible. Cruciferous vegetables, like kale, arugula, broccoli, Brussels sprouts, cabbage, and collard greens, deliver high levels of antioxidants and have been proven to reduce inflammation in the body, an important fact to note, as inflammation is one of the leading causes of disease and advanced signs of aging. These foods also have high levels of vitamins, minerals, phytochemicals, and fiber.

EF: In your book, Younger, *you suggest people follow a particular diet for younger-looking skin. What is your advice to those who are vegan?*

HL: With the prevalence of vegan eating, the focus on plant-based proteins has become much greater—but there are still good and bad options. I usually tell clients to avoid soy as it can create excess estrogen in the body and is usually highly processed and not organic. Great, natural options for green protein include lentils, hemp seeds, quinoa, spirulina, chia seeds, and of course, almonds and walnuts, which are rich in healthy fats. Even for a vegan or vegetarian, protein is crucial to overall health and the beauty of skin, and is absolutely something that should be consciously consumed.

EF: As souping is becoming the new healthy habit, what is your take on soups, their soup-er powers, and how that relates to healthy and young-looking skin?

HL: I find souping to be a fascinating health trend; when made at home with beneficial ingredients, soup can be an amazing method of eating many servings of whole, healthful foods in a flavorful and appealing way.

EF: What are your top veggies, legumes, spices, and herbs—for a younger skin—and why?

HL: Cruciferous vegetables are always my first recommendation when asked about nutrition-conscious eating, and using spices like black pepper, cayenne, and cinnamon, or flavoring foods with lemon creates a deliciously healthy and alkaline environment in the body without the use of salt.

EF: How important is soup cleansing to clear skin?

HL: A healthy diet is of paramount importance to clear, radiant skin. If you are eating poorly and leading an inactive life, you could spend a million dollars on treatments and products and it would amount to nothing. Allow your food to create your glow from the inside out. Aim to make gradual changes that become habits over time. You can change your taste buds and your food preferences more easily than you'd think. When you feel good, you look good, and when you look good, you feel even better.

EF: Just as our digestive system takes in food, processes nutrients, and gets rid of waste, our skin takes in nutrients from the blood, produces by-products (like oil and dead skin cells), and sends what it doesn't need back into the bloodstream. Skin has its own metabolism. How do you get gorgeous from every single meal?

HL: Phytonutrients, vitamins, and minerals are all critical to a glowing complexion. Try to include fresh greens and herbs in every single meal. It's easier than it seems. Have an avocado with breakfast, arugula in your salad at lunch, and steamed greens on the side for dinner. Your body will thank you.

ALLOW YOUR FOOD TO CREATE YOUR GLOW FROM THE INSIDE OUT: DR. LANCER'S RX FOR GREAT SKIN

Eat lots of cruciferous vegetables.

Use spices, such as black pepper, cayenne, and cinnamon, or flavor foods with lemon instead of salt.

Try to include fresh greens and herbs in every single meal.

Aim to make gradual changes that become habits over time.

When you feel good, you look good, and when you look good, you feel even better.

10

FIND YOUR SOUP-ER CALM

Thanks for sticking with me until the very end. I'm about to share with you my most secret recipe of all. And it has nothing to do with soup.

You see, until I received my diagnosis, I was your typical hard-nosed, cynical, and practical journalist out there. I made fun of anything New Age, except for a few Enya tracks. I needed proof, science, verification of everything or I wouldn't trust it.

So, naturally, when a friend suggested I see a healer, I thought she'd lost it. Funnily enough, a healer presented herself to me when I least expected it. What she told me stuck in my mind and made me search for answers.

I became obsessed with reading accounts from people who were terminally ill, went to see healers, such as John of God in Brazil, and were then proclaimed cured by their Western doctors. People who were wheelchair-bound would make a pilgrimage to the healing waters of Lourdes in France and arrive home, walking. Even my mother had stories about friends of friends who were cured by Russian healers in remote villages. What was it that turned around all those people's fate? Was it the healer? Or was it them?

How our thoughts and feelings affect the health of our body is not a conversation you have at your doctor's office. Yet doctors know that our mind and body communicate through hormones and neurotransmitters that originate in the brain and then leave the brain to signal other parts of the body. We all know of the "placebo effect," but why are we not connecting the dots? If we get better by simply believing it, why don't we incorporate this into a treatment plan?

Positive feelings of hope, love, gratitude, and belief in ourselves strengthen our immune system and can heal our body. And guess what? There is science behind it. Lucky me, I had teachers appear in my path and guide me to recovery without my even realizing it at the time. I was introduced to Kundalini yoga and breathing, mindfulness mediation, and visualization that helped me connect with my soul. And soup was what warmed my soul and blazed the trail to my recovery and optimum health.

Positive Thinking

Have you ever thought about why you think the same thoughts all the time? Where did they come from? And why do you believe them? I call those thoughts "my critics." They might be here to protect me, but sometimes they really mess me up. The more I think about them, the bigger and more powerful they become. A smart teacher who helped me on my healing journey explained to me that if I simply thank those thoughts and replace them with different ones, I will empower myself. She taught me that I should treat my thoughts and emotions as guests, with respect and honor, but that I'm in charge. I know that most of our thoughts are subconscious and we can't always control the first thought that just pops in. However, it is up to us to control our second thought. So, when doubt and negative thoughts come knocking, have a self-talk. You know what I'm talking about: that inner dialogue we all have with ourselves. Pause and say, "Delete," just as you would hit the Delete button on your computer. Then think of anything positive and replace the negative thought with a ray of sunshine. It might take a few times, but practice makes perfect. You would be amazed what you can talk yourself into and out of with the new positive thinking and positive self-talk.

Visualization or Guided Imagery

You've heard it a million times: A picture is worth a thousand words. Visualization is creating a picture in your mind of what you want and putting the power of your intention to work. The more colorful the picture, the more details that are filled in, the more specific the result. Remember, your body will do whatever you believe. What do you see? What do you feel? What do you hear? What does it smell like? And this is not some New Age woo-woo; many studies have validated the effectiveness of visualization and it is even used in hospitals.

Visualization is very powerful in healing because it's pulling the person toward a visualized healthier future. You can do it on your own, in a group setting with scripts, or with a guide. Here is a very simple exercise:

Start by sitting comfortably in a chair or lying down. Close your eyes, start gentle breathing (in through your nose and out through your mouth), relax your muscles, and then picture a part of your body you'd like healed. Imagine vividly that part of your body going through the healing process—whatever that looks like to you; maybe it's your aching knee being warmed by the sun or waking up every morning migraine-free—and then feeling healthy.

Mindfulness Meditation

I'm sure you've been hearing a lot about the power of meditation lately. But with so many techniques out there, how do you pick one? Some meditations are designed to help us relax, others to create an altered state of consciousness; Zen meditation, Vedic meditation, Transcendental Meditation, prayer mediation, Taoist meditation, Buddhist meditation, and many others.

Personally, I lean toward the simplicity of mindfulness meditation and the power of the mantra-driven Vedic meditation.

Mindfulness meditation teaches awareness of everything in our lives: our thoughts, surroundings, and physical sensations. It teaches us to be present and helps us be present with whatever is happening, resulting in a relaxed body and mind. Mindfulness is just the answer for so many of us who are overwhelmed by life and feel that we aren't really living at all. I like to describe it as a mental workout. And who can't use one of those? But seriously, it trains our mind to meditate on things we cannot change, to not try to escape the discomfort but to accept it as part of life. It also provides a simple way to tune in to your brain and calm your mind.

One of my favorite exercises is called "mindful observation," a simple but powerful way to connect to what's around us. Pick something to watch for a few minutes. I like looking at clouds, sunsets, the moon, or just a flower. Notice it as if you are seeing it for the very first time. Notice any emotions that come up and allow your spirit to connect: Don't judge what you see, don't analyze, just be present and aware.

Another exercise I love is practicing silence. Spend a few hours in complete silence. Just absorb your surroundings and be. I like doing this exercise on a plane: I put on my earphones and eye mask, close my eyes, put my hands on my knees, and relax. This really helps with tuning in with what's happening inside you. You can practice silence while eating soup; trust me when I say it's quite meditative. This teaches you how to eat without talking, reading, or checking your phone. When you eat in complete silence, you taste more and eat less. When we are aware of what we eat, we choose the right foods that heal us.

Meditation

with Anand Mehrotra, meditation and yoga master, founder of Sattva Yoga

Vedic meditation is a bit more complicated, so I turned to Anand Mehrotra to guide us through this powerful practice that works on your unconscious. Anand is a visionary meditation and yoga master, and the founder of Sattva Yoga. He runs a center for self-discovery and transformation in Rishikesh, India, but has amassed a huge following in the United States. I met Anand a few years ago during one of his yearly trips and was impressed with his wisdom.

EF: Why is meditation so powerful?

AM: Meditation is the way to master our mind and through that live a more aware and joyous life. The practices of meditation have been around for centuries; they allow us to see who we are beyond all the noise of the world. I think this is the most important lesson we can learn in our time on this planet. Through meditation, we can start to experience ourselves before thought and make contact with the pure field of potentiality. This results in deeper peace and gives us access to a higher dimension of intelligence within us.

EF: It's also healing . . .

AM: Research has shown the deep connection between mind and body. Through meditation the stress levels of the body go down, which naturally helps in creating a healing environment in the body. Moreover, if we have a consistent practice of meditation then we have a great possibility to use the power of conscious attention, visualization, and positive thought to help us heal.

EF: How do you pick a mediation technique that's right for you?

AM: What is important to realize is that ultimately it is not the practice that is meditation but what happens inside you that is meditation. Meditation is something that happens to you when you consistently follow a practice. So, just choose which meditation technique you feel most attuned to and then stay consistent with that practice. Preferably twice a day for at least 15 minutes each. There is no best practice, there is just your practice. It is the sincerity of the practitioner that is more important.

EF: What's your advice on how to stay motivated to meditate twice a day?

AM: Simple. I think people need to take a deep look at what they value most in life. If you value being happy, peaceful and healthy, then you will naturally create time for meditation. It will become an essential natural part of your life.

EF: What are the most common mistakes people make that interrupt their meditation practice?

AM: People keep trying different techniques but never settle for one. It's important for progress to find your practice and then stick with it. Meditation only works when it is a consistent practice. Don't try too hard to meditate; you need to relax and allow it to happen. Remember, just because you feel restless and experience too many thoughts, don't get frustrated or judge yourself. Remember meditation is about love. Love yourself. Love and accept your experience, whatever arises. Let it arise. The stillness in you will become stronger and will help you go beyond the mind.

EF: Can we meditate anywhere?

AM: Designate a specific area in your home for meditation. Make it very comfortable and inviting. Let it be your sacred spot. A meditation cushion to sit on and a meditation shawl (silk or wool) to cover yourself during meditation are useful tools. Pick a time in the morning before you start your day, try to be consistent with this time, the evening time can fluctuate as per your day flows. Evening practice can be after work or even after dinner before you go to bed.

EF: I just read a new study that for the first time proves that meditation alters cancer survivors' cells. This is very exciting because for a long time scientists thought we are all wired for happiness, depression and so on.

AM: What scientists are discovering now the Yogis have known all along. The term neuroplasticity referring to the brain's capacity to develop new synapses is new to the West but in yogic path this was always known. As I mentioned before meditation allows us to go beyond thought. We become aware of the true Self beyond the mind. As we experience this presence, we develop more control over our mind and can direct it where we want it to go. You see, no one wants to be depressed or unhappy, it is our minds that lead us there. So learning to control the mind or master the mind is fundamental to unleashing the mind's creative potential.

Here is a simple, effortless technique that will help you develop a solid mantra-based meditation practice.

ANAND MEHROTRA MANTRA MEDITATION

Get a comfortable seat. You can sit on the ground with a cushion or you can just use a chair. Set an alarm for 15 minutes. Sit up with your spine straight and close you eyes inward. Fully relax into the present moment. Begin to watch your breath fully. Slow, long breath. And now introduce the mantra, "SO—HUM." It means, "I am THAT," "I am what I seek." It is the mantra of truth of life. You are all that you seek. Just let the mantra continue effortlessly within your mind and let the breath flow softly in and out. As thoughts arise simply keep bringing your attention to the mantra and breath. You will soon start experiencing moments when there is no thought and no mantra. You are simply present. Anytime when thoughts arise, come back to the mantra.

Brain Food

with Dr. Daniel Amen, MD, founder and CEO of Amen Clinics, double-certified psychiatrist, and nine-time New York Times *best-selling author*

After speaking with Anand, I knew I had to call on Dr. Daniel Amen, the foremost authority on how our brain works. He is one of my favorite doctors and a pioneer in studying our brain.

I first met Dr. Amen over a decade ago, when I was working at CNN. We flew to his clinic in Costa Mesa, California, to interview him for a CNN Medical in-depth report on his breakthrough treatments of ADD/ADHD. That was the first time I encountered a physician who took medications away from his patients and prescribed diet and lifestyle changes. The medical community was furious with him, but Dr. Amen's passion, knowledge, and most important, the health transformations of his patients have all earned him an honorary spot in the medical Hall of Fame. Dr. Oz called Dr. Amen "one of the most gifted minds in medicine," and I cannot agree more. When it comes to the brain, there is nobody in the world who knows more: Dr. Amen has scanned over eighty thousand brains—that's quite a record!

EF: Do you believe in positive thinking, meditation, and visualization?

DA: I like accurate thinking more than positive thinking. Positive thinking tells people they can eat anything and be healthy. I want my patients to have a bit of anxiety so they make better decisions. I am a huge fan of meditation and visualization.

EF: When I first interviewed you back in 2003, I was very impressed but didn't realize at the time what a visionary you were about the influence of our food and lifestyle on our mental health. When did you first recognize that what we eat affects our brain?

DA: It was the early '90s, after I started looking at the brain. It was clear alcohol and caffeine were bad for the brain but then I realized diabetes, hypertension, and heart disease were bad for the brain, too, and they were all diet-related. I started to eat better, lost weight, and began to learn more and more. There was already science showing that diet mattered to mental health.

EF: I'm so taken by the profound changes you've seen with your patients once you removed them from prescriptions and prescribed a Dr. Amen–approved diet.

DA: The best testimonials we receive at the clinics are from our nutrition department: better mood, memory, focus, weight, gut health, less sickness overall. It can be really amazing. A recent patient from Ecuador lost 70 pounds in one year since coming to the Amen Clinics. Her mood, memory, and focus have been improved; she has been transformed. We also saw so much improvement in her brain scan; she says that the diet saved her life.

EF: How important is proper nutrition to our brain? In your book Change Your Brain, Change Your Life, *you call our brain "the most important real estate in your body." Why?*

DA: Your brain uses 20 to 30 percent of the calories you consume. Proper nutrition is the most important thing you can do for your brain. You can exercise all you want, think all the right thoughts, meditate, and take dietary supplements, but if you continue to eat highly processed foods, laden with sugar, bad fats, salt, and made from ingredients grown with pesticides, flavored with artificial sweeteners, colored with artificial dyes, and treated with artificial preservatives, there is just no way to keep your brain and body working at their peak. If your food is not the best, you will never be your best.

EF: What exactly happens in our brain when we eat well and when we don't eat well?

DA: Poor nutrition increases inflammation, a low-level fire that destroys our organs. Pesticide-laden foods damage the microbes in our gut, which in turn hurt the brain. Poor nutrition increases blood sugar, which damages blood vessels. Poor nutrition makes us nutrient-deficient, so our brain cannot operate. We eat too much sugar and foods that turn to sugar and not enough healthy fats, like avocados, seeds, nuts, coconut oil, and omega-3s.

EF: There's been a lot of research in the past five years about the importance of our gut . . . it's now called our second brain . . . please tell me about the relationship between our gut and our brain.

DA: They are totally connected! Gut microbes make vitamins and neurotransmitters, and support our immune system.

EF: Let's talk soups. I still cannot believe that my oncologist proclaimed me cured after two years, especially since one of my genetic tests showed a high likelihood of return within seventeen months. I know the proof is in the soups I have created and in the complete overhaul of my diet and lifestyle. But since I'm a journalist and you are a doctor, what do you think changed my genetic outcome?

DA: You changed the epigenetic expression of your genes, to help you heal rather than hurt you. I am inspired by your story and wish more people would take control of their health as you did.

EF: How can soups help with healing?

DA: I am a huge fan! The soups provide released nutrients in high doses that are more available for absorption.

EF: I'm thrilled that more and more people are now paying attention to nutrition and consider complementary therapies when they get sick. What would you like to see happen in modern medicine?

DA: Food first . . . do no harm . . . more prevention-based rather than illness-based.

EF: How does our brain health help or hurt our body health?

DA: Brain controls your decisions; your decisions control your health.

Nature

There is a reason for the famous saying "Wake up and smell the roses." Connecting with nature is healing. I love to quote Hippocrates who said, "Nature cures—not the physician." Being in nature is one of the best prescriptions for health. Whether it's the woods, the mountains, or the ocean, time spent outdoors is restorative and relaxing. When you are in nature, you naturally become more self-aware and inspired. It's also a great place for solace, refuge, and clearing your head of life's demands and those disruptive thoughts. Take the time to tune into nature and you will begin to tap into its abundant healing powers. Even if it's a short walk at lunchtime, simply getting outside can brighten your day.

Yoga

The practice of yoga is an important part of any healing journey. But the yoga that chose me was not the physically challenging Hatha, Ashtanga, or Vinyasa, so popular in the United States. It was Kundalini yoga. I began practicing with my friend Terena who brought me to Golden Bridge Yoga, a yoga and spiritual community in LA, sustained by the devotees of Yogi Bhajan, the master teacher of Kundalini. My favorite teacher, Tej (one of the greatest living masters of Kundalini and a student of Yogi Bhajan), gave me a healing mantra I was to chant every day; I learned specific breathing patterns and postures to work on specific issues. It wasn't a body workout many people think about when they hear "yoga"; it's an ancient technique of vocal vibrations and body angles that alter your state of consciousness so that deep healing can take place. This was the place I experienced crying with my eyes closed. My body was cleansing. It still remains one of the most powerful experiences of my life.

Quite a few yoga styles are practiced in the United States today and everyone will gravitate toward the practice that best fits their energy and goals. I suggest taking classes at different studios; you will know when you connect with a teacher. You know what yogis like to say: "When the student is ready, the teacher will appear." *Satnam!*

Breathing

Whether you decide to practice yoga or not, breathing has to become your new favorite friend. "Wait a minute," you say; "what do you mean, 'breathing'?" Most of us are shallow breathers or breath holders. Come on, fess up; this includes you! When you are stressed, what do you do? Hold your breath. You can exhale. Does it feel better? Deep breathing creates a sense of calm in your mind and body, and when you breathe deeply and slowly, you activate the parasympathetic nervous system, which reverses stress responses in your body. And you know what that means? All that oxygen being pumped into your body helps you heal and keeps you healthy.

The Healing Power of Breath

with Tej Kaur Khalsa, Kundalini yoga master, custodian of the archives of the teachings of Yogi Bhajan, founder of Nine Treasures Yoga

Tej taught me everything I know about breathing; she is the one I went to for wisdom on breathing and yoga.

EF: Why is deep breathing important to our health?

TK: No one can live without breathing and yet most people ignore the breath. Yogi Bhajan said that every day we ask for illness and sickness when we do not voluntarily breathe. If you want to succeed in your life and be healthy, your power of breath should be your own power. Normally you breathe fifteen times a minute. If you breathe ten times a minute, you'll be very energetic. If you breathe five times a minute, you'll be very intelligent. If you can breathe one time a minute, you will become invincible.

EF: How can you tell if you are breathing correctly?

TK: First of all, observe the navel point. When we take a breath into the body consciously, the navel point will expand. The entire abdominal area needs to be filled. Second, the chest expands; and third, the shoulders, and collarbone expand up and slightly back. On the exhale, reverse the process: First relax the collarbone and shoulders, then empty the chest, and finally pull in on the abdomen and navel area to force out any remaining breath.

EF: Does changing the way we breathe result in psychological changes in our health?

TK: Shallow breathing makes a person more anxious. The connection to the Universal Prana, or life force, is limited. Subconsciously we feel shut off, and even panicked to a degree. A longer, deeper breath can bring a sense of security to a person. The feeling that we are "connected" to something bigger, brighter, and wiser, which can translate into our own expression in what we do in life is critical, especially in such a hectic world we are living in. The more full we can breathe, the more intelligently we can decide things.

EF: It's fascinating and I know many people don't know this. Kundalini Yoga opened my eyes to the importance of breath.

TK: Kundalini yoga is very powerful: Just one breath, one mantra, or one meditation has the power to change the life and destiny of a person forever. Breath of Fire, for example, when done regularly, will clean the mucus out of the system; it will oxygenate and clean the blood from impurities. It sends purified energy to the organs. Breath of Fire will regulate the pituitary. Pituitary will regulate the entire glandular system. Glandular system will change the nervous system. The nervous system will tell the organic system of the blood to just recapture itself.

BREATH OF FIRE

Breath of Fire is rapid, rhythmic, and continuous. It is equal on the inhale and the exhale, with no pause between them (about two or three cycles per second). It is always practiced through the nostrils with mouth closed. Breath of Fire is powered from the navel point and solar plexus. Begin practicing Breath of Fire for a duration of 1 to 3 minutes. Some people find it easy to do Breath of Fire for a full 10 minutes right away.

+ To exhale, expel the air powerfully through the nose by pressing the navel point and solar plexus back toward the spine. This feels automatic if you contract the diaphragm rapidly.

+ To inhale, the upper abdominal muscles relax, the diaphragm extends down, and the breath seems to come in as part of relaxation rather than through effort.

+ The chest stays relaxed and slightly lifted throughout the breathing cycle.

+ When done correctly, the hands, feet, face, and abdomen should be relaxed, not rigid.

+ If the breath creates an initial dizziness or giddiness, take a break. Some tingling sensations and lightheadedness are completely normal as your body adjusts to the new breath and new stimulation of the nerves. Concentrating at the brow point may help relieve these sensations. Sometimes these symptoms are the result of toxins and other chemicals released by the breath technique. The symptoms may be relieved by drinking lots of water and changing to a light diet.

+ Breath of Fire is not hyperventilation.

+ There are restrictions for doing Breath of Fire while pregnant and menstruating.

Keep breathing!

I Love Me

Loving yourself is an important step in healing. No need to put yourself down and feel bad about how things turned out for you. Lift yourself up and you will be amazed how that will change the course of your life.

Try this with a bowl of soup every day to fall in love with yourself:

+ **Be grateful.** Each morning, express gratitude for the new day and the wonderful things in your life. It will start your day on a high note.

+ **Forgive.** We've all made mistakes; that comes with being human. What lessons did you learn from those mistakes? Forgive yourself and let it go.

+ **Create happy thoughts.** Nurturing positive and loving thoughts actually rewires your brain to produce positive and healing feelings.

+ **Reflect.** Before you go to bed, think about your day and review at least three positive things that happened. You will start noticing how that will create a pattern of goodness and you will set good things in motion.

+ **Believe your thoughts.** Imagine your ideal life. Write down what you want, believe in it, and watch it happen.

The Power of Soup

I always remember the story of the stone soup, a tale of a couple of travelers who come to a village overcome with famine, where the villagers hoarded their food when they had it. These travelers announce they are making "stone soup," and as the villagers hear about the soup being made with just a stone and a pot of water, they come and begin to add their own offerings to the soup to make it tastier for all to enjoy. Soup, to me, means coming together. Soup means family. And now, to me, soup means Soupelina and my warrior mother, who not only fought her breast cancer, but is also setting out to educate and aid anyone and everyone who wants to learn how to live a truly healthy life. Which brings me back to the story of the stone soup, where everyone comes together over something they believed in and, by doing so, made it great. To me, soup is a metaphor for life and society, so it's what you make it.

Spread love and share soup.

XO Madeline

A year ago I made a major decision to completely cleanse and change my life. Soupelina soups aided me in the process of me purifying my body and resetting my mind. High-caliber ingredients, clean recipes, and the knowledge to take control of my own body have all played a massive role in my recovery. Elina Fuhrman has created a concept that is simple yet revolutionary: give your body the nutrients and vitamins it needs to stay strong, focused, and healthy.

—Adam, brand director, West Hollywood

Fact: I love anything that makes my daily life healthier and saves me time and hassle with my nonstop schedule. Which is why when I want to pack in more nutrition in my diet, have a cold, or simply don't have time to prepare meals, Soupelina is an amazing must-have nutritional powerhouse. Enjoy every healthy, delicious slurp!

—Sara, writer, Los Angeles

Each soup is uniquely delicious and healing, truly created with love incorporating the freshest ingredients. The flavors are out of this world; they make me feel better immediately. With Soupelina, I know that I'm loved and that everything will be okay. I love you, too, Soupelina! Thank you for changing my life and making me a better person.

—Morgan, mother, Los Angeles

As Elina's guest, I had the privilege of shopping and watching her prepare meals but she didn't just prepare meals, she had ceremonies and rituals in honor of the food. This passion was beyond my expectations and I know that everything that went in my mouth was blessed with her energy and respect for whole foods. After 5 days [of soups] my body was transforming from the inside out. I felt healed, like my body was saying "thank you" for the soups, juices, and all the other special meals. Anything Elina touches is worth the rave. I wanted Elina to adopt me and take care of all my nutritional needs. Thank you, Elina!

—Rose, psychologist, New York

After the first day of the Soupelina 3-day cleanse, I felt energized and ready to take on the next two days of cleansing. Day two was a bit more difficult, though ending the day made me feel even more grateful for my soul, mind, body and will-power. After day three, I was glowing from the inside out! Soupelina delivers delicious soups and results on your overall mental, spiritual and physical health.

—Kelly, genetic counselor, Valencia

I was skeptical; Soupelina said I could lose 3 pounds in 3 days. Don't get me wrong; I love soup, and all things cleansing, but I had never done a Soup Cleanse. Just as she promised, I lost 3 pounds in 3 days! It was easy, and I wasn't even hungry. Three soups and two broths per day kept me full and surprisingly satisfied. Her special blends are nutritious and hearty, and they're packed with loads of flavor. I'm not talking about the boring canned stuff here, I'm talking about delicious sustenance that aids in digestion, maintains metabolism, and makes your skin glow!

—Amby, entrepreneur, Beverly Hills

I never thought that I could get so much satisfaction and an explosion of flavors from a soup until Soupelina arrived on the scene. Elina's loving attention to every ingredient that she puts in her magic soup potions are a dose of good energy. Every time I have one of her extraordinary soup blends, I feel a nurturing warmth of goodness.

—Shivangi, yogini, New York

I was in Los Angeles for several surgeries and staying at a hotel. The discovery of Soupelina was a godsend! I had three days of healing nutritious soups delivered to my hotel room. I was looking forward to my soups and loved the variety. I felt so good that I couldn't believe my body has been through so much. When my doctor saw me for my post-op appointment, he was surprised that I had no bruising anywhere. I attribute that to the healing powers of Soupelina's soups. When I get back home, I'm definitely getting on the Soupelina cleanse again! I feel happy, full of energy and light!

—Ava M.

I'm not a soup person. I never buy it or order it in restaurants. Yet, somehow, Elina's magical concoctions have changed my mind about soup. Hers are not at all "soupy" but delicious and satisfying. I never thought I would find myself enjoying soup this much.

—Cynthia, theater owner, Los Angeles

METRIC CONVERSIONS

The recipes in this book have not been tested with metric measurements, so some variations might occur.

Remember that the weight of dry ingredients varies according to the volume or density factor: 1 cup of flour weighs far less than 1 cup of sugar, and 1 tablespoon doesn't necessarily hold 3 teaspoons.

GENERAL FORMULA FOR METRIC CONVERSION

Ounces to grams	multiply ounces by 28.35
Grams to ounces	multiply ounces by 0.035
Pounds to grams	multiply pounds by 453.5
Pounds to kilogram	multiply pounds by 0.45
Cups to liters	multiply cups by 0.24
Fahrenheit to Celsius	subtract 32 from Fahrenheit temperature, multiply by 5, divide by 9
Celsius to Fahrenheit	multiply Celsius temperature by 9, divide by 5, add 32

VOLUME (LIQUID) MEASUREMENTS

1 teaspoon = ⅙ fluid ounce = 5 milliliters

1 tablespoon = ½ fluid ounce = 15 milliliters

2 tablespoons = 1 fluid ounce = 30 milliliters

¼ cup = 2 fluid ounces = 60 milliliters

⅓ cup = 2 ⅔ fluid ounces = 79 milliliters

½ cup = 4 fluid ounces = 118 milliliters

1 cup or ½ pint = 8 fluid ounces = 250 milliliters

2 cups or 1 pint = 16 fluid ounces = 500 milliliters

4 cups or 1 quart = 32 fluid ounces = 1,000 milliliters

1 gallon = 4 liters

LINEAR MEASUREMENTS

½ in = 1 ½ cm	10 inches = 25 cm
1 inch = 2 ½ cm	12 inches = 30 cm
6 inches = 15 cm	20 inches = 50 cm
8 inches = 20 cm	

VOLUME (DRY) MEASUREMENTS

¼ teaspoon = 1 milliliter

½ teaspoon = 2 milliliters

¾ teaspoon = 4 milliliters

1 teaspoon = 5 milliliters

1 tablespoon = 15 milliliters

¼ cup = 59 milliliters

⅓ cup = 79 milliliters

½ cup = 118 milliliters

⅔ cup = 158 milliliters

¾ cup = 177 milliliters

1 cup = 225 milliliters

4 cups or 1 quart = 1 liter

½ gallon = 2 liters

1 gallon = 4 liters

WEIGHT (MASS) MEASUREMENTS

1 ounce = 30 grams

2 ounces = 55 grams

3 ounces = 85 grams

4 ounces = ¼ pound = 125 grams

8 ounces = ½ pound = 240 grams

12 ounces = ¾ pound = 375 grams

16 ounces = 1 pound = 454 grams

OVEN TEMPERATURE EQUIVALENTS, FAHRENHEIT (F) AND CELSIUS (C)

100°F = 38°C

200°F = 95°C

250°F = 120°C

300°F = 150°C

350°F = 180°C

400°F = 205°C

450°F = 230°C

ACKNOWLEDGMENTS

I'm so grateful I have an opportunity to thank people who have helped me, guided me, stood by me, and cheered me during this process. I would have never made it this far without you.

Thank you from the bottom of my heart:

To my agent, Cassie Hanjian, for finding me, believing in me, and convincing me to do this book thing. I'm so grateful for your incredible spirit and beautiful energy. Because of you, I'm now able to help so many more people embark on a journey to health. I feel so lucky you came into my life.

To my editor, Renée Sedliar, for your patience and unwavering support. Thanks for steering this ship and for being such a cheerful captain.

To Dr. Anthony Bazzan, for your generous support of my work and the rad foreword.

To my wonderful and soup-er talented photographer Pär Bengtsson, for these stunning and inspiring images that make my soups look yummy.

To Randy Price, art director extraordinaire, for believing in the Soupelina power and driving all the way from New Mexico (with Chloe Belle) to direct the book.

To Angela Yeung, the über-talented food stylist, for making each bowl look like art and for teaching me a trick or two.

To my daughters, Madeline and Isabelle, for being my biggest cheerleaders and soup tasters, and for reminding me to trust my gut. For picking up veggies from the farmers market, for watching my soups, for delivering, for helping me pick up quirky and fun soup names, and for Instagramming my culinary madness.

To my amazing mother, Rita Kozmits, the original mad scientist in the kitchen, for your love and for always telling me that I can do anything.

To my grandmother Freida, *babushka*, who is no longer with us but who was the one who taught me the importance of healthy eating.

To my BFF, Amby Longhofer, for always being there for me through thick and thin: for wiping my tears during my tough decision-making about my medical treatments, for all your help with Soupelina, and for encouraging me when I needed that extra-special Amby touch.

To the incredible Robert Seidler, for validating my work, for giving me confidence to launch Soupelina, and for moving mountains for me. I'm overflowing with gratitude for how much you and Alecia have supported me.

To my dear friend Terena Eisner, my most Zen friend and such a shining light, for always helping me pull it together and for reminding me that I can do it.

To Dr. Kristi Funk, for giving me the gift of knowledge. I will always be grateful for the time you've spent with me explaining everything and answering all my questions. And for always being available and loving, despite your busy schedule and a set of triplets.

To Dr. Mao, for your wisdom, talent, heartfelt guidance, and generous support of my health, my work, and me.

To Dr. Gez Agolli, for being authentic and for always having answers; for sending me late-night e-mails to make sure I feel better and have all the information and tools.

To Dr. Philomena McAndrew, for being the patient support throughout my treatments and for going outside of your comfort zone for me when I would throw my unconventional treatment ideas on you.

To Angela Rukule, for giving me the confidence to find myself.

To Liz Mahoney, for planting a seed in my head that I can feed people, not just my family.

To my friend Valerie Gradury, for opening my eyes on cancer, for bouncing ideas, and for being a really cool gal.

To my friends since forever Catherine Lorenze and Nonnie Preuss, for always being just a phone call away and giving me the confidence I needed.

To my friend Elinor Tatum, who kicked my ass when I spent weeks crying and feeling sorry for myself after receiving the cancer diagnosis.

To all my wonderful experts I interviewed for this book: Dr. Gerard Mullin, Dr. Daniel Amen, Dr. Harold Lancer, Tej Kaur Khalsa, Martha Soffer, and Anand Mehrotra, for trusting me with your wisdom and being generous with your time.

To the glam squad, Kristiee Liu and Yvette Beebe, for making me look gorg for the book photos, covering up my under-eye bags, and making my mane look luscious.

To stylist Brandi Jones for dropping whatever you were doing to come and pick out clothes for Madeline, Isabelle, and me, so we can look great in photos.

To Jennings and Lilly, my sweet Cavalier King Charles spaniels, for being the best dogs and confidants. For sitting on my lap, for licking my face, and for being such loyal pooches when I didn't know whether I was going to make it.

And finally, to my customers and everyone who has ever wanted to be healthy but didn't know how. This is for you!

REFERENCES

What Should I Eat?

Nonorganic veggies and fruits: The Environmental Working Group (EWG) found that up to 98 percent of all conventional produce, and particularly the type found on its "dirty dozen" fruits list, is contaminated with cancer-causing pesticides. Accessed at http:www.ewg.org/foodnews/list/.

Milk: D. David Ludwig and Dr. Walter Willett's study in *JAMA Pediatrics*. Accessed at http://archpedi.jamanetwork.com/article.aspx?articleid=1704826.

GMOs

Health dangers of GMO corn: Study by University of Caen, Gilles-Eric Seralini, lead researcher, *Food and Chemical Toxocology* journal. Accessed at http://www.forbes.com/sites/jonentine/2012/09/20/scientists-savage-study-purportedly-showing-health-dangers-of-monsantos-genetically-modified-corn/.

Dangers of GMOs: Nineteen studies. Accessed at http://www.enveurope.com/content/23/1/10.

Processed Foods

Microwave popcorn: The US Environmental Protection Agency (EPA) recognizes the perfluorooctanoic acid (PFOA) in microwave popcorn bag linings as "likely" being carcinogenic, and several independent studies have linked the chemical to causing tumors. Similarly, the diacetyl chemical used in the popcorn itself is linked to causing both lung damage and cancer. Accessed at http://www.drweil.com/drw/u/QAA400701/Microwave-Popcorn-Threat.html.

BPA still widely used in canned goods: Accessed at http://www.scientificamerican.com/article/bpa-still-widely-used-in-canned-goods/.

The dangers of French fries: "Should I Eat French Fries? Scientists Weigh In on the Risks," *Time* magazine. Accessed at http://time.com/3896083/french-fries-potato/.

Beneficial Foods

Mushroom benefits: Research by Japan's Kisaki Mori, PhD, from the Mushroom Research in Tokyo. Accessed at http://www.mitoku.com/products/shiitake/healthbenefits.html.

White button mushroom research: Beckman Research Institute, City of Hope, California. http://www.cityofhope.org/superfoods-mushrooms.

Dandelion properties: University of Maryland Medical Center. Accessed at http://umm.edu/health/medical/altmed/herb/dandelion.

Lime properties: Y. Miyake, A. Murakami, Y. Sugiyama, et al., "Identification of Coumarins from Lemon Fruit (Citrus Limon) as Inhibitors of In Vitro Tumor Promotion and Superoxide and Nitric Oxide Generation," *Journal of Agricultural and Food Chemistry* 47, no. 8 (August 1999): 3151–57.

Sesame oil study: *American Journal of Clinical Nutrition* study found that the risk of colorectal tumors decreased by 13 percent and the risk of colorectal cancer decreased by 12 percent for every 100 mg of magnesium taken in. Accessed at http://ajcn.nutrition.org/content/early/2012/07/31/ajcn.111.030924.abstract.

Bitter melon as treatment for diabetes: Accessed at http://www.sciencedaily.com/releases/2008/03/080327091255.htm.

Nuts sidebar: http://www.nytimes.com/2013/12/18/dining/are-nuts-a-weight-loss-aid.html?_r=0, http://livehealthy.chron.com/intestinal-problems-caused-eating-nuts-4974.html.

Detox symptoms: http://biovedawellness.com/2010/02/the-herxheimer-reaction-feeling-worse-before-feeling-better/.

Gut health: http://www.mprnews.org/story/2015/06/09/bcst-microbes-gut-bacteria.

Organic produce vs. nonorganic: *Journal of Applied Nutrition* 45, no. 1 (1993): 35–39.

Newcastle University study led by Prof. Carlo Leifert, published in the *British Journal of Nutrition*, http://www.ncl.ac.uk/press.office/press.release/item/new-study-finds-significant-differences-between-organic-and-non-organic-food.

Grape leaves powers: http://www.healwithfood.org/health-benefits/eating-grape-vine-leaves.php.

Potty Talk

R. E. B. Tagart, "The Anal Canal and Rectum: Their Varying Relationship and Its Effect on Anal Continence," *Diseases of the Colon and Rectum* 9 (1966): 449–52.

Sakakibara Ryuji, Department of Internal Medicine, Division of Neurology, Sakura Medical Center, Toho University, Sakura, Japan. "Squatting, Influence of Body Position on Defecation in Humans." Accessed at https://vw-squattypotty.storage.googleapis.com/uploads/2015/03/03/files/Japanese-study.pdf.

Dietary Fiber

M. A. Pereira, E. O'Reilly, K. Augustsson, et al., "Dietary Fiber and Risk of Coronary Heart Disease: A Pooled Analysis of Cohort Studies, *Archives of Internal Medicine* 164 (2004): 370–76.

E. B. Rimm, A. Ascherio, E. Giovannucci, et al., "Vegetable, Fruit, and Cereal Fiber Intake and Risk of Coronary Heart Disease Among Men," *JAMA* 275 (1996): 447–51.

L. Brown, B. Rosner, W. W. Willett, and F. M. Sacks, "Cholesterol-Lowering Effects of Dietary Fiber: A Meta-analysis," *American Journal of Clinical Nutrition* 69 (1999): 30–42.

M. B. Schulze, S. Liu, E. B. Rimm, et al., "Glycemic Index, Glycemic Load, and Dietary Fiber Intake and Incidence of Type 2 Diabetes in Younger and Middle-Aged Women," *American Journal of Clinical Nutrition* 80 (2004): 348–56.

S. Krishnan, L. Rosenberg, M. Singer, et al., "Glycemic Index, Glycemic Load, and Cereal Fiber Intake and Risk of Type 2 Diabetes in US Black Women," *Archives of Internal Medicine* 167 (2007): 2304–9.

W. H. Aldoori, E. L. Giovannucci, H. R. Rockett, et al., "A Prospective Study of Dietary Fiber Types and Symptomatic Diverticular Disease in Men," *Journal of Nutrition* 128 (1998): 714–19.

C. S. Fuchs, E. L. Giovannucci, G. A. Colditz, et al., "Dietary Fiber and the Risk of Colorectal Cancer and Adenoma in Women," *New England Journal of Medicine* 340 (1999): 169–76.

Protein and fiber: Marla Reicks led the study on fiber at the University of Minnesota in St. Paul.

Center for Science in the Public Interest. Accessed at http://www.cdc.gov/nutrition/everyone/basics/protein.html protein requirements.

Fiber-cancer protection: D. M. Klurfield, "Dietary Fiber-Mediated Mechanisms in Carcinogenesis," *Cancer Research* 52, no. 7 (April 1, 1992): 2055s–59s.

Soupelina Secrets—Make It Your Soup Cleanse

Infrared saunas: Dr. Oz, http://www.livestrong.com/article/240539-infrared-sauna-benefits-risks/.

http://www.wellnesshour.com/2012/08/22/benefits-of-a-far-infrared-sauna/.

Massage research: http://www.wsj.com/articles/SB1000142405270230453790457727730 3049173934.

Dr. Michael Galitzer, in Suzanne Somers, *Knockout*, p. 216. According to the National Center for Complementary and Alternative Medicine (NCCAM), part of NIH, in 2007, 3.1 million people tried acupuncture, a million more than in 2002.

Recipes References

Soak Up the Sunchoke

The October 2008 issue of *Food and Chemical Toxicology* published a study to investigate antiproliferative effects of chicory in cancer. The researchers focused on four human cell lines, including breast, prostate, kidney, and skin cancers. They found that chicory showed a selective antiproliferative activity on melanoma. They concluded that toxicity of the plant was irrelevant for human health and chicory treatment of melanoma was highly sensitive and cost effective.

You Say Tomato, I Say Yellow Tomato

A study by Ohio State University, published in the *International Journal of Food Sciences and Nutrition*, says that antioxidant benefits of yellow tomatoes may be greater than red tomatoes due to the stereochemistry of the molecule tetra-cis-lycopene that our body digests much easier that trans-lycopene from the red tomatoes.

I Don't Carrot All What They Say

Journal of Agricultural and Food Chemistry 48, no. 4 (April 2000): 1315–21.

http://www.ncbi.nlm.nih.gov/pubmed/10775391.

World's Healthiest Foods, Carrots

With My Chick-a-Peas

Anticancer vitamins and minerals: Source: M. S. Donaldson, "Nutrition and Cancer: A Review of the Evidence for an Anti-Cancer Diet," *Nutrition Journal* 3 (2004): 19, doi: 10.1186/1475-2891-3-19.

What the Hemp?

Carol S. Johnston, PhD, Cindy M. Kim, MS, and Amanda J. Buller, MS, "Vinegar Improves Insulin Sensitivity," *American Diabetes Association Diabetes Care* 27, no. 1 (2004): 281–82.

Brave New Watermelon

Agricultural Research Service study by Agnes Romano, research chemist at the ARS Natural Products Utilization Research Unit in Oxford, Mississippi, in collaboration with plant physiologist Penelope Perkins-Veazie of ARS South Central Agricultural Research Lab in Lane, Oklahoma. Accessed at http://www.ars.usda.gov/is/pr/2003/030221.htm.

http://hortsci.ashspublications.org/content/46/12/1572.full.

Macho Gazpacho

Study by Antonio Martin from the Nutrition and Neurocognition Laboratory at the Jean Mayer USDA Human Nutrition Research Center on Aging at Tufts University in Boston, Massachusetts. Published in the *Journal of Nutrition* (November 3, 2004).

INDEX

recipes using, 101, 103, 106, 109, 110, 116, 118, 121, 122, 125, 127, 131, 136, 137, 140, 142, 146, 149, 154, 158, 160, 163, 166, 179, 180, 182, 187, 188, 195, 197, 200, 201
Garlic mincer, 37
Gattefossé, René-Maurice, 72
Gilberg-Lenz, Susanne, xvi
Ginger
    about/benefits, 47, 187, 195
    recipes using, 101, 104, 116, 125, 160, 163, 167, 171, 179, 180, 182, 187, 195
Glycemic index definition/description, 18
GMOs, 18, 210
Grape leaves
    about/benefits, 43, 146
    finding, 147
    recipes using, 146
Gratitude, 5, 78, 226, 238
Greiner, Lori, 13
Gut/balance
    bowel movements and, 217, 218, 220
    gut as "second brain," 12, 215–216, 233
    gut health "prescription," 220
    importance of, 11–12, 215–219
    listening to gut, 215, 219
    microbiome of, 215, 216, 218, 219
    Mullin on, 217–220
    prebiotic foods and, 218, 219, 220
    sleep and, 218, 220
    soups/cleansing and, 219
    See also Digestion

Gut Balance Revolution, The (Mullin), 217

Hahnemann, Samuel, 27
Harissa
    green harissa topping, 149, 150
    recipes using, 139, 149
Healers, 225–226
Healing
    loving yourself, 238
    overview, 225–236
    See also specific components
Health
    as choice, xvi
    taking responsibility for, 20
    See also specific components
Herbs
    growing/drying your own, 48–49
    types overview, 50–52
Herxheimer effect, 59
Herxheimer, Karl, 59
Hing spice, 180
Hippocrates, 11, 29, 43, 215, 217, 234
Homeopathy/naturopathy
    cancer and, 28
    overview, 27–28
    questions/answers, 28–29
    soups/soup cleansing and, 29
    spice mix and, 29, 30
    strengthening immune system, 28
Hyperbaric oxygen therapy (HBOT), 74

Imagery, guided, 227
Immune system
    homeopathy/naturopathy and, 28
    sickness and, 12–13